IMAGINE EMMA

FriesenPress

One Printers Way
Altona, MB R0G 0B0
Canada

www.friesenpress.com

ISBN
978-1-03-831401-7 (Hardcover)
978-1-03-831400-0 (Paperback)
978-1-03-831402-4 (eBook)

1. FAMILY & RELATIONSHIPS, DEATH, GRIEF, BEREAVEMENT

Distributed to the trade by The Ingram Book Company

IMAGINE
Emma

A father's grief journey

RICK JOHNSTON

Table of Contents

Unable are the Loved to die /
For Love is Immortality

— Emily Dickinson

Foreword

BY JOE SIDDALL

Like Rick and Frances Johnston—and tens of thousands of other Canadian parents—my wife and I lost a child. In February 2014, our son, Kevin, died after a six-month battle with cancer.

When such tragic events happen, a dividing line in every parent's life occurs: life before and life after. In the moment, through the tears, anger, grief, sadness, and countless other emotions, each of us is changed dramatically forever. How can we not change?

So many things are beyond our control, but we can control how we move forward.

As Yogi Berra once said, "When you come to a fork in the road, take it."

But which way?

That simple three-word question is layered in complexities.

My wife, Tamara, and I didn't know how to deal with grief. Most people don't, initially. You're thrust into so much pain, and such deep, uncharted waters.

Fortunately, we are blessed with a tremendous support network of family and friends in Windsor, Ontario.

From Kevin's diagnosis in the summer of 2013 until his death, we spent virtually every day with him in a London hospital. There were ups and downs, good days and bad days.

Through it all, we did our best to concentrate on good news and positive vibes. It wasn't easy.

Being a doctor herself, Tamara was a rock. I leaned on her, heavily. She understood what the doctors were saying and would often have to translate their words into layperson's terms for me.

By Christmas, it was apparent Kevin's courageous battle with non-Hodgkin's lymphoma was approaching its denouement. We knew it. Kevin knew it. And his older siblings, Brooke, Brett, and Mackenzie, knew it.

When the inevitable did come, we agreed as a family that our path forward was to always strive to feel gratitude for the time we had, not miserable about what might have been.

Or, as our daughter Mackenzie coined, "an attitude of gratitude" for the almost fifteen years we had with Kevin. It's easier said than done, but it never stops us from trying.

Everyone grieves differently. There are no right or wrong answers. There is no one-size-fits-all road map to follow to get you through such heart-wrenching tragedy.

In this book, Rick Johnston opens up as a father, husband, and human being—one can feel his raw emotion, even years later—as he sprinkles humour and positive messages amidst stark reality in hopes of helping others who are enduring similar pain and tragedy.

Rick's journey offers some comfort and hope to other bereaved parents.

Joe Siddall, a former Major League Baseball catcher and current television analyst for the Toronto Blue Jays, lives in Windsor with his wife, Dr. Tamara Siddall.

Dedication

This book is dedicated to my grandchildren
Audrey and Archer, and any other young ones who
may come along, because they remind us every day of the
joyful, playful, and unconditional love that toddlers provide.
Peak-a-boo, you two!

Section One
Anguish

Mostly it is loss which teaches us
about the worth of things.

— Arthur Schopenhauer,
nineteenth-century philosopher

Chapter 1

Imagine Emma

More than twenty-five years later, the early morning hours of March 6, 1998, are in my head and vivid as ever. The pain-laden primal scream from my wife, Frances, upon discovering the lifeless body of Emma, our precious two-and-a-half-year-old. The call to 911. The paramedics, police, and social workers. The hospital, then the funeral home, the church, the burial.

Even today, as if on a video loop in my head, the images replay over and over if I let them.

On that cold March morning, Frances and I entered what I call the "fraternity of the unthinkable."

Until you lose a child, it's inconceivable for parents to think about it. Why would anyone contemplate that? You'd drive yourself mad. Or, as my good friend Dan Bailey says, "just the thought of it gives you a shiver."

But once you lose a child, it's difficult to think of anything else for a very long time.

It's a fraternity fraught with tears, broken hearts, life adjustments, and unbearable loss.

And yet, I'm not unique. So many others have been forced into a world of living—and parenting—after the death of a child.

On average, six Canadians under the age of fifteen die every day—or 2,200 every year, according to Statistics Canada. Note that this number includes deaths from all causes, including illness, accidents, and other factors.

So, today there are six more fathers like me, six more tomorrow, and six more every day beyond.

Since Emma's death, 55,000 other Canadian children under age fifteen have died. That's equivalent to the population of Fredericton, the capital of New Brunswick. That's more than 110,000 bereaved parents in Canada.

(Age fifteen was selected because the child is typically dependent and living at home, but that does not in any way mitigate the amount of pain and suffering associated with losing a child at any age, whether eighteen, twenty-eight, or forty-eight.)

I can honestly say that over the ten thousand days that have passed since her death, not one day has been without a thought, or multiple thoughts, about Emma. Indeed, on many rainy days, when I'm feeling blue, I find myself at Emma's gravesite, standing over our Johnston family tombstone thinking of what might have been.

This book is one bereaved father's story about life and parenting after the death of a child. Others were impacted by Emma's death, too, not just Frances and me. Foremost would be our three other daughters—Kasia, Amanda, and Melanie—whose lives also suddenly changed.

The horrific loss of our child still looms large in all our lives, especially mine.

Immediately after Emma's death, I shifted into "Super Dad" mode for the sake of the family. I also buried myself in work to try to distract myself from the crippling grief that would roll over me if I let it. For years, I saw a first-rate psychologist, Dr. Louis Cannella, until his retirement in 2021.

Though he diagnosed me with depression, I chose talk therapy, not prescription drugs. Pills have their purpose, but they aren't for me. I witnessed the negative effects meds had on my sister Brenda, who died three weeks before Emma on Valentine's Day, 1998.

Some, including my family, have questioned why I've undertaken this project so many years after Emma's death.

Before answering, let me first cite an international expert in the field of grief and bereavement:

"Your head knows time; your heart doesn't," says Dr. Stephen Fleming, professor emeritus in the Department of Psychology, Faculty of Health at York University, co-author of *Parenting After the Death of a Child*, and sought-after speaker all over the world on the subject of losing a child.

Dr. Fleming also says, "Grief is not short term and finite. The time dimension doesn't matter, especially with the death of a child."

Beyond that, I hope my story can help or give comfort to anyone in the fraternity of the unthinkable.

And I hope it provides clarity to our children and grandchildren on why I did this or that. Everybody parents differently. There is no road map laying out what to do after the death of a child. I did my best. Frances did her best.

And, yes, I made mistakes. But I did what I did out of love, rarely anger.

To be honest, my anger—when it appeared—was aimed at God more than anybody or anything. Why did He allow this to happen to such a young and innocent girl? I've tried to live an honest, hard-working existence, doing unto to others . . ., so why was I subjected to such pain and cruelty? I'm sure other bereaved parents in the fraternity know what I'm talking about. Over time, any anger dissipated, and I stopped blaming God.

I also hope that writing from a father's perspective proves beneficial to both dads and moms. Fathers are wired to be protective of their children. Mothers are too, of course. Beyond the trauma and pain, one comes to realize we cannot fully protect our children. It's a bitter pill of stark reality to swallow.

It's the reason I became hypervigilant and overly protective with our three other daughters. If it could happen to one, it could happen to others. As I said, I wasn't operating with a road map, let alone a GPS, to take us to the right places all the time.

When Emma died, we didn't just lose a wonderfully jovial person whom we all loved. We also lost the years of promise—Emma's future—that we so looked forward to as parents.

In bereavement, there is no one-size-fits-all solution for easing the pain.

Frances and I were like two country roads that would intersect at times, but we were definitely going in different directions at other times. We each had to do different things for different reasons.

Even today, for example, when Frances thinks of Emma, she pictures her solely as a little girl.

I, on the other hand, always picture her in various stages of life. I imagine Emma graduating from grade school, high school, and university. I imagine Emma as a teenager and going to her prom. I imagine Emma as an aunt, wife, and mother.

That's all I can do: imagine.

Aptly, the day Emma died, the number-one song in North America was "My Heart Will Go On" by Celine Dion from the hit movie *Titanic*.

I am, and always will be, a father of four—not three.

What follows is one dad's journey.

For no soul can ever be replaced,
and death claims a beauty and a
magnificence that will always be missed.

— JOCELYN SORIANO,
BESTSELLING AUTHOR AND POET

Chapter 2

Parents' Worst Nightmare

Just days before Emma died, Frances had an unsettling dream. When she awoke, she nudged me in bed next to her and was quite agitated and near tears.

"I dreamt I was at a funeral," Frances said. "But I couldn't tell who died. I kept asking people, 'Who is it? Who died? Why are you so sad?' No one answered me. I couldn't make out what it was all about other than sadness was everywhere; I could feel the overwhelming sadness."

That morning, I tried to comfort Frances by telling her the dream was likely brought on by my sister Brenda's funeral two weeks before.

Frances was unconvinced, but at the time she didn't think it was a premonition about Emma or any of the girls, just a really bad dream. Nor did I imagine it was a sign of impending doom. Why would I? Parents can't live continually thinking the worst could happen to their child or children. But the dream was upsetting to both us, especially Frances.

A parent's worst nightmare is most definitely the loss of a child. It can cause long-lasting emotional and psychological trauma and your world is divided into "life before" and "life after" the loss.

Frances and I had met in September 1974 at the University of Toronto's Mississauga campus. We were both studying urban planning, with my minor being English literature and Frances's sociology. After a few weeks, I screwed up the courage to ask her out. On October 20, we had our first date at Villa Borghese, now called ViBo, an Italian restaurant at Royal York Road and Bloor Street.

ViBo's food is great, but more importantly, they had a piano player (and still do). The romantic in me thought the place would impress this young lady.

Frances was slim and proceeded to eat a healthy amount. (She's always been slim and seems unfamiliar with weight gain; whereas I have a never-ending battle of the bulge.)

I was a twenty-year-old student, and all I had on me was cash; there were no credit cards for kids back then. About halfway through dinner, I realized I might not have enough money. "Uh-oh," I thought to myself. "I will be washing the dishes tonight if she keeps eating!"

In a nervous, squeaky voice, I discreetly leaned toward Frances and said, "I might be a little short, do you have any cash on you in case I need it to avoid washing dishes?"

She smiled and nodded. As it turned out, I had enough cash to cover the bill, and Frances said she thought it was cute that I was so honest. All in all, it was a very successful evening!

At university, we had some classes together and our professors knew we were dating. From that point onward, we were a couple.

Frances and I were married on October 15, 1976, at the Old Mill, a picturesque and rustic inn and conference centre on the banks of the Humber River in Etobicoke. The week before, I had turned twenty-two. And two weeks before, Frances had celebrated her twenty-third birthday. We were very young and very much in love.

It was a charming wedding with sixty guests, mostly family and a few friends from high school and university. My dear dad had died three years before, and I remember wishing he had been there that day. Being from a large family, Frances's parents were not paying for the wedding, nor did my widowed mother chip in. I'm proud to say we paid for and arranged the entire event ourselves.

To keep costs in line, I even made the invitations on a clunky old computer at work and printed them off. In the summer of 1976, I had a temporary student job doing clerical work with the provincial government.

Our wedding day was such an important day in my life that I can remember it like yesterday. The wedding ceremony was in the chapel at 6 p.m. It was dusk and candles were lit in the chandeliers.

Frances looked beautiful in her white-hooded wedding dress, and she was rocking a Maggie Trudeau-style curly hairdo. I, on the other hand, looked pretty silly, but it was the times. I wore a then-trendy baby blue tuxedo jacket with navy pants and a blue shirt with navy ruffles. Just to round out the mid-'70s look, I had long hair and a beard. Years later, whenever our daughters looked at our wedding pictures, they'd giggle and announce that we looked better now than on our wedding day! Oh, to be young again and get a do-over. I would have dressed better.

At the Old Mill, we had four dozen coral- and peach-coloured Sonia roses in plain vases on stands at the front of the chapel. A United Church minister officiated, and I remember Frances's dad giving her a hard time about the wedding not being Catholic. The service was followed by a cocktail reception and a seated dinner in the Mill Room.

At dinner, a lovely glowing fire was burning in the fireplace and lit candles were everywhere around the room. Everything felt perfect.

We spent our wedding night at Toronto's Harbour Castle Hotel in a suite overlooking the lake. Not bad for a young couple still in our early twenties.

Unfortunately, the stress of the wedding led to Frances getting laryngitis, making our short four-day honeymoon in Montreal quiet, yet still very special. My only regret was that we flew to Montreal instead of taking the train. It would have been more relaxing, less hectic, sitting on the train for five hours sipping champagne and talking about what was ahead for us. Oh, well. As I said, we were young.

We settled into marital life quite easily. Despite studying urban planning at university, I decided it wasn't for me and landed a permanent Ontario government job. I started at the Toronto Assessment office in September 1976, one month before the wedding. I set my sights on being a real estate appraiser, not an urban planner.

Frances also pursed a career with the Ontario government, but at the Ministry of Municipal Affairs and Housing. Frances has always had a head for numbers and, armed with a CPA (Chartered Professional Accountant) designation, her job entailed approving and processing payments from the provincial government to municipalities.

(Frances comes by her head for numbers honestly. Take, for example, the number seven. Frances was the seventh delivery for her mother, who lost four children in Poland after World War II. Seven was her mother's favourite number, and she died on August 7. And our girls' times of birth all ended in sevens: Kasia, 10:17 a.m.; Amanda, 5:37 a.m.; Melanie, 3:17 p.m.; and Emma, 11:57 a.m. Frances can recite all these numbers and dates off the top of her head!)

With our careers just getting going, we took our time before having children. Almost a decade after our wedding, Kasia was born, soon followed by Amanda. Six years later, Melanie arrived.

It was after Amanda's birth in July 1986 that I decided to become a real estate agent. By this time, I was an accredited appraiser through my role with the Ontario government. Being an appraiser was a real benefit when I charged into a new career in real estate sales and joined RE/MAX in 1987. Careerwise, I've never looked back.

But on a personal level, a year or so after Melanie's birth in 1991, I got it in my head that I really wanted a fourth child. Frances, who had turned forty by this point, was not so sure. She was content and, initially, wanted to stop at three daughters. But I kept at her, saying things like a fourth child would make a wonderful symmetrical family unit. It took some doing on my part, but my perseverance paid off and Frances agreed.

At forty-one, Frances was pregnant once more. When we told the three girls, I remember Kasia saying we were "too old" to have another child. We chuckled and hugged the girls. It was a great time in our lives, both at home and in our careers—me selling real estate and doing better than I'd imagined, Frances flourishing in the provincial civil service.

It was almost too perfect as I had the flexibility to be around during the day to do drop-offs and pickups at school. Frances could be home in the evenings while I'd be out showing homes to clients or working on purchase offers and other necessary parts of the real estate agent profession. We also had help with household cleaning, meals, and childcare to fill any gaps when Frances or I were needed elsewhere.

On November 17, 1995, Emma Rachel Natalie Johnston was born. She was pink, rosy, chubby, and adorable.

Kasia, eleven, Amanda, ten, and Melanie, four, all adored their baby sister from the start. Kasia and Amanda were about a year apart and grew very close while growing up. I think Melanie sometimes felt like a third wheel with her older sisters. She immediately bonded with Emma, who was closer to her age.

Quite frankly, the influence Emma had on all of us was enormous, almost from the moment we brought her home from the hospital to our house on Reigate Road, near Dundas Street and Royal York Road in the west end of Toronto.

She was roly-poly, with a crescent-moon smile on her face at all times. Of the four, she was the only daughter to have Frances's blue eyes. Kasia and Melanie were petite and fine-boned like their mother; Amanda and Emma were bigger, like their father.

One thing about Emma that really stood out was that she had a heightened sensitivity about her. Frances recalls how she could sense your mood, and if you were blue, she'd come over and cuddle.

I remember when the other girls would fight or bicker, like sisters sometimes do, and Emma would put herself in the middle of the fracas, break it up, and help everybody calm down. She was a peacemaker by nature and a happy child who didn't ask for much.

A charmer, in the very best sense of the word, Emma could melt hearts with one simple look.

She was also so thoughtful; her consideration for others was far advanced for a child her age. One time in November 1997, just before her second birthday, a little boy at nursery school grabbed one of her cookies. Instead of crying, yelling, or making any sort of fuss, Emma went up to an adult supervisor and quietly asked for another cookie. Instead of eating it, she took it to the little boy who had taken hers, figuring he needed cookies more badly than she did.

"Who reacts that way?" Frances asked at the time. "I wouldn't do that. I would have gone and fought for my stolen cookie!"

A month later, the six of us went to Disney World in Orlando. All the girls loved that Christmas-season trip. Emma was so sweet and in her element. I remember her sitting atop my shoulders during a parade in the Magic Kingdom. She appeared to love the view from that vantage point, and it seemed like every character in the parade's procession was looking and waving at her! That made her smile and giggle.

Emma could also be stubborn as a mule and you knew what was on her mind, even before she could talk. For instance, she hated winter with a passion. I still smile thinking about Frances wrestling with Emma to get her snowsuit and boots on.

Earlier that year, Emma had contracted croup, a common viral illness in children. Croup causes swelling of the throat around the vocal cords and trachea (windpipe). The swelling in the throat can cause a harsh cough that sounds like a seal's bark.

She spent a night in hospital with croup. We followed up by taking her to a specialist who examined her and said she'd grow out of it like most children. Since she was susceptible to that seal-bark cough, we placed a vaporizer next to her bed.

Emma went to nursery school two days a week. On March 5, 1998, our housekeeper at the time, Rosa, took Emma to school that morning and I picked her up in the afternoon. Driving her home, she began to cough. Damn it, I thought, and I took her home immediately.

First, I called our family doctor, Dr. Muriel Henderson, who told me to get her out into the cold, fresh air, and make sure the vaporizer was on in her room that night so she could get a good night's sleep. The doctor was not overly concerned and that made me feel better.

I then called Frances. She had a hair appointment booked after work and wouldn't be home for dinner, perhaps not even before Emma's bedtime. Frances agreed to reschedule the appointment and come home immediately after work.

Once Frances was home, we talked about taking Emma to the hospital. But Frances and I decided together that given what the doctor said we would not take her that evening and make sure she was comfortable in her own crib. Frances then went upstairs and gave Emma a bath.

Hindsight is 20/20. Had we known then what we know now, we would have taken her to the hospital emergency.

There is no silver lining, but I'm glad we made that decision together. Had one of us made the decision alone, the other could have played the blame game. (An upcoming chapter will delve more deeply into the "woulda, coulda, shoulda" issues on a marriage after the death of a child.)

I have a memory that night of Emma standing in her crib and laughing at something silly Melanie was doing to entertain her. Just thinking about that sends tears rolling down my cheeks. Back in those days, Melanie would sometimes sleep in the bed next to the crib, the bed that was to be Emma's and which she never had the opportunity to use. For whatever reason, perhaps wanting Emma to get a good night's sleep, Melanie decided to sleep in her own room that night.

By 11 p.m., the house was quiet and we were all in bed. We checked on Emma before retiring and she looked angelic as she slept with the vaporizer humming in the background.

At 4:30 a.m., Frances awoke to check on Emma. It's best if I let Frances describe the scene:

"I looked from the door and there was what appeared to be spongy vomit stuff around her. She was in the fetal position. My first reaction was fear and hoping she didn't choke on that stuff.

"As I leaned into the crib, I knew she was dead. I tried opening her mouth, but rigour mortis had already set in and I couldn't. I then screamed and screamed, waking up Kasia and Melanie. Amanda was away on a grade 7 class trip that night. I then rushed back to Rick and said: 'Emma is dead. Our Emma is dead.'"

I awoke in shock. Frances says I was like a zombie for the first minute or so. As anyone can imagine, it was bedlam.

Kasia, who was in grade 8, was quick to respond and immediately called 911. An ambulance and the police were dispatched, and the operator asked someone to try mouth-to-mouth resuscitation. Our thirteen-year-old Kasia did it. Both Frances and I regret being unable to do this, but we did not have our wits about us at the time.

In only minutes, police, an ambulance, and an eight-months-pregnant social worker were at our house.

Everything happened so quickly.

"How does this even happen?" Frances says to this day. "There's such a fine line between life and death, and I never thought—until that moment—that the line could be so tenuous."

As the two paramedics tried in vain to resuscitate Emma's lifeless body, two police officers escorted us out of her room and downstairs, along with the social worker. I said to the cops, "Ask away. Ask us anything. I know how this works. My dad was a cop."

One officer was male, older, and seemed to be in charge. He asked all sorts of questions. The other officer was younger and female. They were both courteous. In fact, Melanie remembers the female officer reading a bedtime story to her in the family room while we talked to the other officer.

The older cop gave the impression that he'd experienced scenes like this before. The younger one appeared a little agitated, possibly upset seeing our baby girl. But who knows for sure? She did have the wherewithal to distract Melanie and read her a story. I was in a haze, so I could have read her body language incorrectly. When a police photographer arrived, she took him upstairs to Emma's room, where he took many pictures, while the older cop continued asking us questions.

Police have to investigate cases like this to make sure nothing untoward occurred. We were okay with that and were, frankly, still in a state of shock. I will say that exactly one week later to the day, the male officer phoned Frances and started asking how she was doing. He quickly pivoted to more detail-oriented questions. He left Frances with the impression that he wasn't convinced it was a natural death, which still bothers me to this day.

About a half hour after arriving, the paramedics loaded little Emma's body into the ambulance and took her to the hospital morgue. I rode with them, at least I believe I did, but I cannot say for sure. My mind and, therefore, my memory, was jumbled badly for several hours. Frances was driven by the pregnant social worker after our neighbour Brenda Gibson graciously hurried over to look after Kasia and Melanie until we returned.

We were met at the hospital by our family doctor, who was visibly shaken herself. We were taken in to officially identify the body. There on the slab was our little girl, or at least her body.

Frances leaned over and hugged Emma. Whether because of the coldness of Emma's body, the trauma of the event, the shock, or whatever, Frances let out these ear-piercing primal screams. I went to console my wife, and one of the doctors took my arm and said, "Let her scream. She needs to do this."

This medical professional intrinsically knew that emotional release is important and should never be discouraged. The moment to deal with emotions is when they are experienced, not postponing them until a more convenient time or place can be sought out. I wish I knew then what I know now, but life doesn't work that way.

After Frances regained some composure, we insisted on an autopsy. Even in that state of mind, we both knew we had to know exactly what happened to our beautiful little girl.

The autopsy was conducted and days later we learned that time of death was 1:30 a.m., three hours before Frances's discovery. It also stated the cause of death was asphyxiation, and it was labelled "a natural death." There was no mention of croup in the autopsy report.

We returned home around 8:30 a.m., our lives forever changed.

You don't have to see the whole staircase,
just take the first step.

— MARTIN LUTHER KING JR.

Chapter 3

The First Year
without Her

Arriving home from the hospital morgue that morning, I was surprised to learn six-year-old Melanie insisted on going to school that day. For her, being with her grade 1 classmates was a normal thing to do amidst the most abnormal of days.

As for me, I was still in a daze. We all were. But little Melanie felt a need to tell her teacher all about what happened, including telling her about the police officer who read her a story early that morning. Looking back, Mel handled this the best of all of us initially. Perhaps it was her tender age and not yet being equipped to deal with or understanding exactly what had just happened. I don't know.

"I was very insistent that I go to school that day," Melanie says today. "I remember a lot from that time. I'm surprised I still have such vivid memories."

I've read (and heard) in many places that the first year after the death of a child is often the most difficult for parents and family members. I'm skeptical of that. The first year—with its shock, pain, and raw emotion—is the most intense, but all the following years are difficult.

As a father, I still had three surviving children and a wonderful wife. I could not afford to wallow in grief. I took it upon myself to keep my family together. I went into Super Dad mode almost from the moment we arrived home from the hospital. I was determined not to turn into a recluse floundering in pain.

I didn't know the path forward, but I did know that sitting on the couch watching that movie of pain play over and over again in my head served no one. Not me. Not my family. Not my friends.

When longtime friend Dan Bailey reflects back on my reaction, he says, "Rick has worked extraordinarily hard not to let this be the cardinal compass point for his life, and especially for his surviving children. I hope what comes through loud and clear in this book is that Rick has been a loyal, supportive friend to many, many people since Emma died. Kindness is a gift that gives in both directions, and I think it has helped Rick as he grieves while, at the same time, spreading his kindness."

The author of *Peter Pan*, J. M. Barrie, a literary expert on never growing up, once said something poignant along these lines: "Always try to be a little kinder than is necessary." It's easier said than done, especially after losing a child, but well worth remembering.

The grieving process is different for everyone but judging by the books I've read and the people I've spoken to about it, there are some common experiences many people go through.

First, in the immediate aftermath of the death, parents can feel a sense of shock and disbelief. It is beyond difficult to accept that your child is gone and come to terms with the reality of the loss. As Frances said, the line between life and death is often tenuous and can be erased as easily as children's chalk on the sidewalk after rain.

Second, all parents experience a range of intense emotions during the first year after the death, including, but not limited to, sadness, anger, guilt, and despair. We certainly experienced that, and these emotions can be overwhelming at times and come in waves.

"Virtually every time a child dies, there is trauma complicating the grief," says Dr. Stephen Fleming, the internationally recognized parental bereavement expert. "Your assumptive world is destroyed. Parents assume they can protect their children. But these deaths force parents to acknowledge that we can't protect our children. When a child dies, that goes Kaboom! It's gone."

Dr. Fleming is so right. Emma's death wasn't anybody's fault, so I don't have guilt but something more like remorse. But when it comes right down to it, I didn't protect Emma. That is one tough pill to swallow.

Third, oftentimes physical symptoms emerge. Things like fatigue, headaches, gastrointestinal problems, hair loss, weight loss, changes in appetite and sleep patterns, ulcers, allergies, or blood pressure elevations can appear. These symptoms make it difficult for parents to take care of themselves and to cope with the demands of daily life.

In the days following Emma's death, a few of my real estate agent friends told me to take some time off, but I couldn't. I found I needed work more than ever.

There were many mornings when I simply wanted to pull the covers over my head and stay in bed. Instead, I forced myself to get into the shower, clean up and shave, put on a suit, get into real estate mode, and play the role of the professional.

In the first few months after Emma's death, I found work allowed me to forget about things for a few hours each day. By the end of each of those days, I was a wreck. I often found myself crying uncontrollably in my car. By the time I arrived in our driveway, I had forced myself to pull things together before heading into the house to face Frances, Kasia, Amanda, and Melanie.

Frances and I dealt with the first year much differently, and I will get into more detail about that in the chapter specifically about the marital impact.

But I will say here, and without any judgment, the impact on Frances was far more profound that first year than it was on me. She was incapacitated with grief, took six months unpaid leave from work, stayed in bed much of the day, and sobbed inconsolably many times per day. Looking back, I repressed the impact initially by moving into Super Dad mode and using work to keep me busy and defer my overarching pain to parts of each day.

Those three general experiences I mentioned above are some of the strongest learnings we had to cope with, but there were others that I'm sure most bereaved parents have dealt with, too. Briefly, here are some more.

The death of a child can be an isolating experience, as friends and family members may not know what to say or how to offer support. It's easy to feel alone and disconnected from others.

Triggers and reminders, such as birthdays and favourite holidays can bring up intense feelings of grief and loss. Other triggers include everyday experiences such as seeing children of a similar age to Emma or hearing a particular song.

Perhaps the most intense example of this happened at a family get-together several months after Emma's death. Our niece Taylor, the eldest daughter of Frances's sister Sarah, flipped her hair back just like Emma used to do.

Immediately, my eyes met Frances's eyes. Without a word between us, I knew we were thinking the exact same thing.

"I need some fresh air," I announced. "Frances, let's go for a walk around the block."

Outside, Frances said to me, "Did you see how Taylor flipped her hair?"

I nodded. We embraced and both started crying in each other's arms.

It would be five long years before Frances could even hold a baby. That came in April 2003 when Taylor's little sister, Kate, was born. Seeing Frances cradle Kate in her arms brought tears of joy to my eyes.

Another aspect to touch upon is how bereaved parents search for meaning in the loss of their child and struggle to make sense of what happened. This is a difficult and ongoing process. Don't expect answers is the best advice I can give.

These experiences are not unique to me. Looking back, that first year after Emma's death was a time of intense grief, emotion, and adjustment. To believe this ends after a year is naïve and misleading. It is also a time when parents need support from friends, family, and professionals who can help them navigate the grief journey and find ways to cope with their loss.

Despite insisting on going to school the day Emma died, Melanie stayed only a few minutes because she found it too hard. Our neighbour Brenda Gibson, who had driven her, waited in the office while providing details of the day's tragic events to the principal.

"I remember walking into class and my grade 1 classmates were all singing the national anthem," Melanie says. "I just burst into tears as soon as I walked in."

Her teacher comforted her, and they walked together to the principal's office where Brenda was waiting. Then they came back home.

Amanda was still away on her overnight winter camping trip with her class to Albion Hills Conservation Park in Caledon, about an hour northwest of downtown Toronto.

The bus pulled up to the school around noon and my friend Gwen Fitzgerald was there waiting for Amanda. Gwen and I would often carpool when delivering and fetching our kids, so when she graciously offered to bring Amanda home, I was thankful.

"I had a feeling something was up," Amanda says today. "I didn't know what, but the teachers were treating me differently on the bus, and then when Dad wasn't there at school, I thought that was strange, too."

On the drive home, Gwen asked Amanda about the camping trip and that was the extent of the conversation. When they arrived home, Amanda saw a white florist's truck in the driveway.

"I knew something was going on, for sure, by this point," Amanda says. "When I opened the door, I saw lots of people in the kitchen, and then Kasia blurted out 'Emma is dead.'"

After being buffeted by the news, Amanda says she thinks she turned and ran out of the house. "I could be mashing together different days, but I'm pretty sure Lisa Truant [one of the girls' caregivers] caught me and consoled me. Those days all became a bit of blur."

There is little point trying to rationalize my actions the day Emma died. I can't explain why I did some things. I just did them.

For example, I went shopping at Sherway Gardens to buy two necklaces, each with a locket. My brother-in-law Eugene, who is married to Frances's younger sister Judy, took me. He drove as I was in no condition to be behind the wheel of a car.

One necklace was for Amanda, and one was for Emma. It was Amanda and Eugene's idea. She wanted something to remember Emma. Amanda's locket holds a picture of Emma, and Emma is buried with the necklace with Amanda's picture in it.

Privately at the funeral home before guests arrived, Eugene helped Amanda put the locket around Emma's neck. He is a lovely man, and I am indebted for that help. I simply didn't have the strength to help Amanda with that task.

Amanda's locket is one of her most precious possessions and remains a reminder of what Emma means to her.

"She was the purest form of love," Amanda says today. "To have experienced her—even for such a short period of time— contributed to who I am today. She wasn't given the chance, so how can I not live my life to the fullest? How can I waste that when she wasn't given the chance?"

And Amanda is not just saying that with the clarity that time and growing older can sometimes provide. She always felt that way. Here is a note I saved that Amanda—only eleven years old at the time—wrote days after Emma's passing: "Emma made all of us laugh and be happy. . . . No one is as special as our little sister. We know she was a gift to us, and she'll always light up my life, wherever I happen to be. I'll never forget her as long as I live because she was so special to me."

Emma's funeral was at 2 p.m. the following Monday, March 9, at Kingsway-Lambton United Church in Etobicoke.

After moving to Reigate Road in Etobicoke, we initially stayed at Windermere United Church and every Sunday we would pick up and drive an elderly parishioner, Lillian Rose, with us. She was so full of life despite the hardships thrown at her. Though Lillian didn't speak of it, her eighteen-year-old son, Douglas, had died in a tragic accident in 1950. The girls all loved Lillian and she loved our girls.

Lillian died on July 24, 1996, eighteen months before Emma. Around that same time, my friend Dan Bailey, the rector of Windermere, left the church to become a teacher. It was at this point we decided to move to Kingsway-Lambton United Church. By chance, Emma was the last baby baptized by Dan before he left the ministry.

At the funeral, Dr. Jan Huntjens was the presiding minister. Atop the coffin was a picture of Emma in a frame that was adorned with pansies, Lillian's favourite flower. Lillian's granddaughter, Judith Champagne, who, coincidentally, was a teacher at the girls' grade school, gave us the picture frame knowing how much we all loved Lillian.

Although Dan was no longer a minister, I asked him to read Psalm 139. The passage expresses the pervasive presence of God that offers us hope and comfort in the face of adversity, trial, and pain. I also asked Dan to say a few words.

The first thing he asked was for everyone in church to hug the person beside them. "God's love is revealed through mighty deeds and tender mercies," Dan said.

Then Dan spoke of our family, Emma's place in it, and Lillian's special bond with all of us. "I can picture Emma and Lillian walking hand in hand in Heaven," Dan said.

The love I felt in the church that day was so powerful and remains in my heart. In fact, Frances remembers a spiritual feeling of love all around her. Another of my real estate friends, Heather O'Regan, commented to Frances after the service that Frances appeared to have an aura of light glowing about her.

"It was really weird," Frances says. "I was in so much pain, but I felt so much love all around me."

Though I didn't know Dr. Jan Huntjens as well as I know Dan, his eulogy was simply perfect.

None of us wanted to hear pious religious messages like "it's God's will" or "God must have had a good reason for taking Emma so young." Instead, he used the word "absurdity" multiple times to describe what happened.

"God, too, is silent, speechless, and powerless in this absurdity," said Dr. Huntjens. "This is a God of love, not a God of death."

He talked of God, like all fathers, picking up sleeping children from the couch or the car's backseat and taking them to their own warm bed. These were comforting images for me and my family.

Later, at the interment at nearby Park Lawn Cemetery, watching our baby go into the ground was the most difficult thing I've ever experienced. We were all in so much pain.

My eyes were red and puffy, and my vision impaired by tears, but as I looked down the row of headstones directly perpendicular to Emma's grave, there was the headstone of Lillian Rose. I had been a pallbearer at Lillian's funeral and at her gravesite, but I didn't realize she was buried that close to the Johnston family plot I purchased.

This was a strange coincidence to be sure, but it was not the last unexplainable oddity following the death of Emma. Regardless, seeing Lillian's headstone and remembering what Dan had said in church about Lillian and Emma walking hand in hand gave me a warm feeling as Emma was being entombed in the snow-covered, cold earth in March of 1998.

And speaking of coincidences, another emerged some months later while I was having lunch with George Demeter, a friend and fellow real estate agent. He told me the story of his daughter Natalie, who died of a brain tumour at age four in 1980. It was devastating for both him and his wife, Kata, also a real estate agent. I had no idea they had been through what we were going through.

"We never advertised or sought sympathy for losing our daughter," George says. "But I felt I needed to tell Rick."

The next time I visited the seventy-three-acre Park Lawn Cemetery—with more than 22,000 graves—I found Natalie Demeter's headstone. Coincidentally, like Lillian, Natalie is also buried near Emma. Indeed, the three graves are all about seventy-five paces from each other, forming a virtual triangle. And inside that triangle is the grave of journalist and radio and TV personality Gordon Sinclair, his wife, Gladys, and their eleven-year-old daughter, Jeanne. Gordon spoke often on CFRB radio about the loss of Jeanne. Anyone can be an unwitting member of the fraternity of the unthinkable.

As for the triangle, the three-sided figure is one of the most symbolic shapes in both our natural and human-made world, especially when it comes to spirituality, religion, enlightenment, and a higher state of being.

Perhaps the most common symbol of the triangle in a religious context is Christianity's Holy Trinity. It represents God the Father, God as the Son (Jesus), and God as the Holy Spirit. By no means is the symbol restricted to Christianity. In Buddhism, the triangle is a symbol for enlightenment and access to higher knowledge through focused concentration and living a composed and calm life. In Hinduism, the triangle is used as a tool to channel certain energies for the purposes of enlightenment and spiritual progression.

Beyond religion, the triangle symbol has been debated for thousands of years— by ancient philosophers and Egyptologists to today's psychologists, architects, and mathematicians. If you ask a psychologist what it means when you see triangles in your dream, she will likely say something like it points to hidden mysteries, wisdom, and finding balance and harmony within conflicting aspects of your life.

Some believe, like the Egyptians with their pyramids, that triangles represent transformation and change during a challenging time, and a path to everlasting life pointing up to the heavens.

I'm not an overly religious person, but I am spiritual. And discovering that triangle with Emma at the top and Lillian and Natalie at the other corners made me feel a little bit better.

For parents, their children's "firsts" are joyous: first words, first steps, first birthday, first day of school, and so on.

For those parents in the fraternity of the unthinkable, "firsts" turn into "withouts," and they are joyless and painful reminders: first week, month, and year without her; first birthday without her; our first birthdays without her; first Christmas and other holidays without her; and so on and so on.

That first year, there were plenty of "first withouts."

We had a four-day weekend in Las Vegas booked for just Frances and me that happened to be a month after Emma's death. Neither of us wanted to go, especially Frances.

After some thought, I proposed we push ourselves and go to Vegas. I remember telling Frances that Emma would have wanted us to go. I thought the change of scenery would be good for both of us.

"I was devastated, but I went, and I'm glad I listened to him," Frances says. "I remember we went to a Diana Ross show and one of the Motown [backup] singers was staring at Rick the whole show. He loved the attention. And I remember talking to another couple in Vegas who told us they'd lost a child, too."

It was our first trip without Emma. It wasn't easy and it wasn't all fun and games. But it was also our first real steps in this new world where we could now only imagine Emma.

Vegas was a nice distraction, but certainly no remedy for our broken hearts. We returned home still in tremendous pain, realizing no matter how much we yearned for the old life with Emma there was only this strange and difficult new life ahead for us.

Every day, for the first six months, Frances and I would walk to the cemetery, pay our respects, and afterwards either go for coffee or stop at the Swiss Chalet on Bloor Street at Royal York Road. Emma and I often went there for lunch, just the two of us.

Some days, we'd take helium balloons filled with messages of love for Emma, and Frances, Kasia, Amanda, Melanie, and I would release the balloons and watch them float off into the sky.

We sought professional grief counselling—individually for Frances and me, and once as an entire family. After the first family session, all three girls said they were not interested in continuing. "You two need the counselling, not us," said fourteen-year-old Kasia. I must admit that comment made me laugh, not angry.

Frances fired her first grief counsellor after a couple sessions. The woman wanted Frances to burn Emma's clothing, give away other precious belongings, and stop "blaming God" for what happened.

"This woman was crazy," Frances says. "I wasn't blaming God. Good grief, therapists should listen and allow the patient to come to his or her own conclusions. But the experience taught me that even when you're weakened and in lots of pain, you have to stick up for yourself."

Frances switched therapists, found it helped, and saw the new person for several years.

Lisa Truant, one of our children's caregivers, spent many days helping Frances write thank-you notes to all the people who attended the funeral and who sent food and other gifts. This included those who generously gave to the Emma Johnston Memorial Fund we established to help less privileged children go to summer camp or to provide financial assistance to help with their education. The fund grew, and over the years it has offered other ways to continue Emma's legacy and help others less fortunate.

Despite the weight of despair, I was constantly reminded of the beauty in humanity. Neighbours dropped off at least a month's worth of dinners at our house. We received so many heartfelt letters and calls from people. Each one carried a similar theme: Emma was a joy who made people laugh with her singing, dancing, and jovial nature. Letters came from parishioners and ministers at Kingsway-Lambton United, Emma's nursery-school teachers, real estate agents, clients of mine, and so many friends.

Such expressions of love and support cannot be overstated in their importance, regardless of the child's age or circumstances of the death.

Here's some simple advice for someone offering help to a bereaved parent: Use the deceased child's name, express to the parent why he or she was special to you, and give a hug.

I remember a young couple, David and Cathy Anderson, who were clients and had just bought a house through me when Emma died. They had three little boys of their own and not a lot of money at the time. Yet, they gave me a bag of food for the family. Such nice people. There were so many wonderful people like them.

My friend Natalie Kotyck, another RE/MAX agent, came over to the house and told me it was time for us to go for a walk. That first walk turned into a daily walk with Natalie for a couple weeks after the funeral. The two of us still walk together weekly and have for the last twenty-five years, except for a brief time when she went to Poland to teach English for a year and a half.

"We didn't talk about Emma at first," Natalie says today. "Then Rick began discussing Emma's death and its impact on everyone in the family. The first big topic was what they were going to do about that first Christmas. I've always said Rick is my best friend. Anything we tell each other will never come back to haunt either of us."

I found walking so therapeutic. The exercise. The talks. The companionship. In fact, it was so good for me that I started walking with Dan Bailey, too. And we still walk together almost every weekend.

Exactly one month after Emma's passing, we received a letter from Michael deBraga, Amanda's teacher who was with her and the class at that winter camping trip in Albion Hills.

"I cannot shake from my memory the sense of desperation and total emptiness that I felt upon hearing the news," Michael wrote on April 6, 1998.

The school phoned deBraga to tell him the news as the class was having breakfast and before returning to Etobicoke that morning.

"I could not help but think of how I would have felt if something had happened to my four-year-old daughter, Inez," Michael wrote. "At the same time, seeing Amanda and knowing that this day would forever change her life was difficult for me. Here, in front of me, was an eleven-year-old girl enjoying a wonderful time with her friends and soon stark reality would strike at her like a sudden chill."

Initially, the letter re-enforced and re-awakened the Super Dad mode in me. If it could happen to one daughter, it could happen to the others. At the funeral home a month earlier, I made a point of talking to all the best friends of Kasia, Amanda, and Melanie and asking for their help in keeping an eye on each of my girls.

It was irrational to expect little girls to understand what I was asking or, God forbid, that they spy on their friends and report to their father. As you'll read, over the years I hovered too much over the girls, particularly in their important teen years. But it was all done out of love and a father being protective. While reading Dr. Fleming's book *Parenting After the Death of a Child*, I discovered my actions were not crazy, but quite normal and predictable for a bereaved parent.

I trust and hope that today Kasia, Amanda, and Melanie all know I did things out of love and caring, never spite or harm.

There were so many other important things occurring during that first year without Emma. The first came on one of our daily walks to the cemetery when Frances turned to me and said, "Emma's not really here, it's just her mortal remains." We no longer needed to continue that daily walk.

Then, not long after that, Melanie went over to Frances, who was sitting on the couch, staring off solemnly. Mel placed an index finger on each side of Frances's mouth and pushed her lips upward.

"Mommy," Melanie said, "it's time for you to smile again."

Out of the mouths of babes, I thought, while fighting back tears.

Of course, Melanie would soon drop a bombshell on me, too.

She and I were having lunch at McDonald's, and at the next table was a young mother and her toddler daughter. Melanie looked at the woman and nonchalantly said, "I used to have a sister who looked just like your daughter. She died."

With a surprised look, the woman turned to me and said, "Is that true?"

I nodded in the affirmative, my eyes puffy and red, but I managed to hold back tears. It was yet another stark reminder that we now occupied a life we didn't want, but we had to get on with it and make the best of things.

October was challenging. It is usually a month of celebration. But October 1998 was more bitter than sweet. Frances's forty-fifth birthday (October 5), my forty-fourth birthday (October 9) and our twenty-second wedding anniversary (October 15) were all muted that year. Each day was a reminder of the former life we longed for, not the reality.

And finally in 1998, there were two more incredibly difficult days.

The first was November 17, which would have been Emma's third birthday. That was one tough day. Oh, by the way, remember the unexplainable coincidences I mentioned in Emma's story? Our first grandchild, Kasia's daughter Audrey, was born on November 17, 2019.

The other really hard day was Christmas. We talked about going away and being out of the Reigate Road house where Emma died, but in the end we decided to stay home.

For such a joyous day of celebration, all five of us were morose thinking about Emma the Christmas before and why she wasn't there with us now. We were all so blue that for the next ten years or more we were away on family holidays at Christmas, usually in sunny places.

Perhaps the first year after the death of a child is the toughest, but, quite frankly, they're all difficult. Frances has her own unique take twenty-five years later: "Rick is frozen in pain," she says. "I hope this book helps him thaw."

Section Two

Acceptance

The soul would have no rainbow,
had the eyes no tears.

— NORTH AMERICAN
INDIGENOUS PROVERB

Chapter 4

Marital Impact

I've found there are many myths surrounding the death of a child and the gaping hole it leaves in loved ones' lives afterwards. The myths vary and include: the impact on parents is different depending on the age of the child; grief lasts two to five years after the death of a child; and fathers conceal their grief more than mothers.

The previous chapter briefly dealt with one myth: If you make it through the "firsts"—essentially the first year after the death—everything will start to improve. I can unequivocally state that this is absolute bullshit. Time does not heal all wounds. Pain and grief do not magically disappear the day after the first anniversary of your child's death—or even after the second, third, fourth, or fifth anniversary.

This reminds me of the words of Dr. Fleming: our head tells time, but our heart does not. While it is true that time can provide a certain level of comfort and perspective, it can never bring your child back and erase all the pain.

And don't get me started on the big "C" for bereaved parents: closure. Such expressions imply moving on and detachment from Emma. I am a father of four, not three, and always will be. Instead of closure, I believe (from my experience) most bereaved parents want to find new ways to emotionally attach to the deceased, not wipe her and the memories away. Death ended Emma's life, not my relationship with her.

This chapter tackles perhaps the biggest myth: the death of a child ultimately leads to divorce for the parents. It's untrue. Don't believe it.

So, where and how did this myth originate? It may have sprung from a journalist's book that was published shortly after the culture-rocking decade of the 1960s. Like many myths, there is a tiny nugget of information hidden inside that swelled and morphed into its current, unrecognizable form.

One of the earliest books to openly discuss the death of a child was *The Bereaved Parent* by Harriet Sarnoff Schiff, then a *Detroit News* reporter and herself a bereaved parent who lost her ten-year-old son, Robby, in 1968. The book was published in 1977 and, according to Schiff's obituary, was "the first book to address the issues of parents who survive their children."

Schiff, who died at age eighty-six in 2022, was a remarkable person. After her book came out, and for many years, she and her husband, Sandy, "travelled the world to work with doctors, nurses, funeral directors and psychologists on how to help families whose children had died," as her obituary states. She went on to write several more books, including one about caring for elderly parents.

Stepping back, for thousands of years when a young child died it was not typically discussed openly. Schiff opened the window and must be recognized and applauded for that. For example, Frances's parents lost four children, and the parents of my collaborator, Robert Brehl, lost two young children years before Schiff's book. Neither Frances nor Bob have any recollections of their parents talking about the deaths. Good on Schiff for opening the window, but one seemingly harmless comment in her book has done a lot of damage.

"In fact, some studies estimate that as high as 90 per cent of all bereaved couples are in serious marital difficulty within months after the death of their child," Schiff writes in her book's final chapter, entitled "Bereavement and Marriage."

She doesn't cite her sources, and yet this relatively innocuous statement about marital strain became a divorce "fact" over the past fifty-plus years. People began to perpetuate the notion that 90 percent of all marriages end in divorce following the death of a child.

After Emma passed, Frances and I even had well-meaning people tell us to work hard on our marriage and not let Emma's death end it. Some people even quoted that ridiculous 90-percent number Schiff had tossed out years before.

Such comments and numbers are folly. I've found no empirical data that proves marriages are automatically headed for divorce after the death of a child. And it's damaging for parents to believe that untruth.

Indeed, on a personal level, I would argue the exact opposite is true. Our marriage is stronger because no one else in the world loved Emma as much as the two of us. That bond can never be broken.

For many years, grief experts challenged the myth but there has been too little evidence to unequivocally refute it or prove it. The precise impact of a child's death on a marriage simply hasn't been studied enough. However, I did find some studies that seem to disprove the myth.

Still, as difficult as the death of a child is on mothers and fathers, research has not found a direct link between parental bereavement and increased divorce rates. Indeed, a Finnish study covering 100,000 married couples from 1971 to 2003 found the death of a child had negligible negative impact on marriage, and actually boosted the chances of the couple having another child.

"We find that child loss only modestly influences the divorce risk, whereas its effect on the risk of parity progression is considerable," write authors Fjalar Finnas, Mikael Rostila, and Jan Saarela.

Parents making that decision to have more children are likely not in marriages careening off the cliff. Some, perhaps. But not 90 percent!

And Dr. Reiko Schwab, professor emeritus at Old Dominion University in Norfolk, Virginia, tackled the divorce myth and all the studies surrounding it at the turn of the twenty-first century and found no evidence of higher divorce rates among bereaved parents. She reported relatively lower rates of divorce, less than 20 percent, which coincided with her own anecdotal observations as a grief support-group facilitator for bereaved parents.

Others—including papers published in the *Journal of Nursing Scholarship* and the *Compassionate Friends* journal—also found strong evidence to refute the myth.

"The actual facts bear out that the death of a child usually acts, instead, to polarize the existing factors found in the marriage; hence, some marriages get worse, some get better, some just maintain, and some actually do end in divorce," writes marriage and family therapist Jean Galica on her website Theravive.

com. "Marriages that have sustained the loss of a child through death experience the same valleys and peaks as any other marriage, just in a more exaggerated form. Whether they become better or worse, the one sure thing is that the marriage will never be the same again as it was before the child's death."

After reading the research and living my life, I am convinced the idea of divorce rates climbing after the death of a child is a myth.

The decision to end a marriage is influenced by many factors, including the quality of the relationship before the death, the circumstances of the death, and the ways in which the parents cope with their grief.

Of course, and studies prove, the death of a child puts significant strain on a marriage, and some marriages may not survive the loss. One study published in the *Journal of Family Psychology* found that approximately 16 percent of couples who experienced the death of a child divorced or separated within six years of the loss. A commonly cited study by the international non-profit group The Compassionate Friends found the divorce rate even lower, at 12 percent.

Undeniably, the death of a child is an extremely traumatic experience for both parents. We all grieve differently—just as everyone has a different fingerprint—and there are marked differences falling between genders. And grieving can cause intense emotional distress, such as sadness, anger, guilt, and depression, which can affect any couple's ability to communicate effectively and connect emotionally. But to make the leap that higher divorce rates must follow is simply not true.

It's important to make the distinction between mourning and grief. Mourning is a process following loss, and grief is the price we pay for loving. Neither Frances nor I love Emma any less than we did when she was alive. We will always have grief, but our mourning eventually subsided.

Still, people cope with grief in different ways, and it is common for couples to have different approaches to dealing with the loss of a child. One partner may want to talk about their feelings and seek support, while the other may prefer to process their grief privately or through other activities. These differences can cause tension and misunderstandings.

I can't say we always coped in similar ways or that we communicated honestly and openly at all times. But when things got really dark—and things could get dark—both Frances and I held tight to the compass that pointed to the common truth and would forever: no one loved Emma like the two of us.

Our grief journeys were and are separate, but in tandem. We've been sympatico for the most part, but there have been times through the years when we each had to do different things for different reasons. This book is an example. Initially, Frances was against the idea, fearing it would open up family wounds needlessly. Over time, she's come to the conclusion the process has been good for both me and the family.

And we've both respected the other's actions and beliefs. Initially, Frances was far more distraught than me. Or, said another way, I suppressed my true feelings whereas Frances let the wave of emotions roll over her the first six months. Over the years, things have reversed, and I am far more apt to openly express my emotions about Emma to family and friends than Frances now does. I picture Emma at different stages of life, from the first day of high school and university to starting a career, getting married, and having children. Frances, for the most part, sees Emma as the little girl she was when we lost her.

Emma's death precipitated a change in priorities for me. I had long dreamed of accumulating property, especially rental properties. My goal was to own ten rental homes and duplexes. My grandfather had instilled in me the value of real estate because "they ain't making any more land." I didn't reach ten rental properties but did hit six at the peak. We now own three.

After Emma, real estate holdings and money meant much less to me. Yes, I still like both but owning real estate and accumulating money no longer drive me. Instead, I wanted experiences with and for my daughters Kasia, Amanda, and Melanie, and with Frances. We travelled a lot, especially around the Christmas season, and at least one other trip per year. We dined at many fine restaurants. I even bought a convertible sports car.

With the lesson ensconced so deeply in my psyche that life is fragile, I wanted to live every day to the fullest. Within reason, of course. I still worked hard, and I wasn't going into debt to finance this new lifestyle choice.

Thankfully, Frances was on board, and we rarely fought about spending too extravagantly.

Frances and I spent time with a marriage counsellor, too. This woman facilitated healthy discussions that were helpful to our marriage. My advice to every bereaved parent is to seek marriage and grief counselling. Even if one thinks counselling is hocus-pocus, give it a try. You may be surprised.

We also re-instituted our "date nights." Throughout most of the 1980s and '90s, Friday was a regular date night for the two of us. After Emma, we've often had more than one date per week—if we include lunches.

Here is a quick aside about date nights and strange coincidences that emerged after Emma's death. One of the girls' favourite caregivers, Gabriela Mendl, was on her first date with her future husband, Mark, the night Emma died. Gaby was the first to babysit Emma, when she was only one week old!

In summary, the death of a child does have a significant impact on a marriage, and it's important for couples to seek support and communicate openly with each other so they can navigate the grief journey and move forward together.

I've found communication is the key. And the communication must be interactive and two-way, not simply coming from one spouse.

And my last piece of experiential advice for bereaved couples is to make what I call "The Promise." Frances insisted on The Promise, and I agreed wholeheartedly, along with some ground rules.

*What we once enjoyed and deeply loved we can never
lose, for all that we love deeply becomes part of us.*

— Helen Keller

Chapter 5

Woulda, Coulda, Shoulda

At the time of Emma's death, Frances asked me for "The Promise."

"Rick, promise me that we won't allow this to tear us apart," Frances said in that hospital morgue on the morning of March 6, 1998.

We were both still in shock and pain as we stood over Emma's lifeless body.

"I promise," I said.

Of course, at the time, we both believed the myth that the death of a child inevitably, and almost automatically, leads to divorce. At that moment, with raw emotion coursing through our veins and tears clouding our vision, we both intrinsically knew no two people on Earth loved Emma like the two of us.

And yet, that divorce myth hung over us like the sword of Damocles and, quite frankly, frightened us. Even though we didn't know it at the time, that myth was causing a lot of damage: we'd just lost our daughter and now the myth was making us think we could lose our marriage.

I'm sure many other couples have felt the same way. Looking back with the clarity of 20/20 vision, Harriet Sarnoff Schiff's book was so important for anyone in the fraternity of the unthinkable, but I wish she had never used that 90 percent divorce "statistic" in her final chapter, which seemed to mushroom and become a fact for many bereaved parents.

"I remember reading a book within six months of Emma's passing and turning to Rick and saying, 'not only have we just lost a child, but we have a good chance of getting a divorce,'" Frances recalls today. She can't remember the book's title, but it likely was *The Bereaved Parent* because of the number imprinted in Frances's memory.

Sometime after I made The Promise to Frances, I insisted on some ground rules. First and foremost, we must always remember that Emma's death was a tragedy, and it was no one's fault. Second, The Promise must be a two-way street for it to hold, as it has for the past twenty-five years and more. Blame, I said, cannot be assigned.

The phrase "woulda, coulda, shoulda" is often used to express regret about past decisions or actions that may have contributed to a negative outcome. In the case of Emma's death, it suggests a sense of hindsight and a desire to change the past, which is impossible.

In the death of any child, it is common for parents and family members to experience feelings of regret, guilt, and self-blame. It is easy to believe that we could have done something differently to prevent the death. Such thoughts and feelings are a normal part of the grieving process. They can be a way for parents to try to make sense of the loss and to find some control in a situation that feels out of their control.

But, and this is a very big but, it is important for parents to recognize that they did the best they could with the information and resources available to them at the time. Emma's seal-bark cough returned. We talked to the doctor, who wasn't concerned enough to order us to take her to hospital. We put on her vaporizer in her bedroom. We tried to make her comfortable so she could get a good night's sleep in her own bed. Regardless, Emma died.

All bereaved parents should try to be gentle with themselves and avoid self-blame or self-criticism. With the divorce myth hanging above them, grieving parents sometimes assign blame on themselves or their spouse, regardless of the facts and circumstances.

That is absolutely the wrong thing to do. Therapy can be helpful in addressing these feelings of regret and guilt, and in finding ways to cope with the loss to help move forward. I know counselling, both together and on our own, helped us, especially six months after Emma's death when Frances began questioning me and my actions.

Frances, who was in the depths of her grief, said I should have known Emma needed medical attention and I should have done this or that. Remember, grief is a long and winding process, not an event. Frances was working through things. She questioned why I didn't know Emma was so sick. I reminded Frances we were both home that night. We both checked on her many times, even minutes before we drifted off to sleep.

Through talking, and with the help of counselling, I told her the covenant of The Promise will be broken if she continues to affix blame. Bad things happen. Really bad things happen. We had to reach a point of inner peace and knowledge for The Promise to be kept.

It was also right around this time when I had the best and worst dream about Emma since her death. For months, I had a horror movie playing in my head where it would happen all over again, and again, and again. Sometimes, this movie would be a dream; oftentimes it was conscious thoughts when I was wide awake. It made me feel sick. Talking about it today still makes me feel miserable when I think about that early morning when Emma died.

Then, one night about six months after her death, I had a new dream. This dream started with Frances giving Emma a bath, drying her off, and handing her over to me. I was playing silly fatherly games like peek-a-boo with Emma, and she was laughing and giggling uncontrollably in her bed. Her laughter in that dream made me so happy that I was literally smiling in my sleep.

It was so vivid, so real, just like it used to be on so many nights after her bath. Then I awoke from the dream, and I was so sad. I wasn't sobbing uncontrollably, but I had tears streaming down my cheeks. It was so painful because it felt so real moments before in slumber, but my conscious reality remained.

As one can gather, Frances and I were not in a good place at this point. We both had lost Emma, but our loss was unique to each of us. This simultaneous, but separate, grief was so debilitating. Neither of us had the power or will to meet the other's needs at the time. As my dream indicates, I was longing to wind the clock back to the "normal" days when I was taking care of my beautiful little girl. But I couldn't even tell Frances about the dream for months because I was still angered over the woulda, coulda, shoulda accusations. (For the record, I can't even tell the dream story today with dry eyes.)

Thankfully, and likely because of that bond of shared pain, Frances and I moved past that dangerous fork in the road.

"Woulda, coulda, shoulda can drive you crazy if you let it envelop and define you," Frances reflects today.

Together, Frances and I stopped looking backwards, or even living life stalled in neutral gear. Yes, we still thought about Emma every day, and still do today, but we began moving toward a new life "after Emma."

"The whole family was suddenly restructured. We had to start doing things differently, and how do we do that?" Frances recalls asking. "I'll be honest, it was a real struggle as a family. We had to rebuild our family life with three children, instead of four. The trips (Rick pushed for) did help because they brought the five of us together and brought us joy by creating new memories."

Bereaved parents should be aware that blaming is a common response to loss, particularly when the loss is sudden and unexpected. It can be a way for parents to try to make sense of what has happened and to assign responsibility for the loss. However, blaming is not a helpful or productive way to cope with grief and can actually make the healing process more difficult.

It is important for parents to try to communicate openly and honestly with each other about their feelings and to avoid blaming or accusing one another. They should try to support each other through the grief process and work together to find ways to cope with the loss. Counselling or therapy can be critical in facilitating communication and in finding ways to work through feelings of blame or resentment.

When one parent blames the other, it can put a significant strain on the relationship and can make the grieving process even more difficult. Blaming one another can create feelings of resentment, anger, and guilt, and can lead to a breakdown in communication and support between the parents.

However, it is important to remember that blaming and resentment are normal responses to loss, and that with time, support, and patience, parents can find a way to work through their grief and heal together.

Through talking to psychologists and therapists, and through our own independent research, I've come to the conclusion that there are three major divisions of grief: shock and disbelief, suffering, and recovery, or at least sufficient recovery to once again live with purpose. But there is no stopwatch on each and no discernible amount of time is known and required for each division. The fact is each phase must be walked through.

Even months after Emma's death, we were still in shock and disbelief, but it was getting better. Suffering clearly remained, and over the years the spikes in pain—while still intense—would not be every day. And after the "woulda, coulda, shoulda" was dealt with, I could feel us inching toward regaining a new life of regeneration and purpose.

At the time, it didn't feel like we were making progress. In hindsight, we were.

But we were also acutely aware at the time that we were not grieving in a vacuum.

Every family is like a knitted blanket. Each member is uniquely part of the quilt—woven and bound together. In normal family life, things will fray, maybe even tear, but the blanket remains intact. Its overall comfort and warmth supersedes any frayed corners or superficial tears.

But when there is a violation of the natural order of things, such as the death of a child like Emma, the blanket is cut to pieces and must be stitched back together. And the new blanket cannot be the same, nor should it.

Frances and I needed to ensure Kasia, Amanda, and Melanie's needs would be addressed and sewn into this new blanket.

Now is no time to think of what you do not have.
Think of what you can do with what there is.

— ERNEST HEMINGWAY

Chapter 6

The Sisters

Without doubt, the death of a child profoundly affects siblings, both emotionally and psychologically. And Emma's death had tremendous impact on Kasia, Amanda, and Melanie.

At the time, Kasia was three weeks shy of her fourteenth birthday, Amanda was twelve, going on thirteen, and little Melanie was only six. During the wee hours of March 6, 1998, Amanda was away at camp and Melanie was so young she couldn't fully grasp the enormity of the situation. Being the oldest and giving mouth-to-mouth resuscitation to Emma on the 9-1-1 operator's command surely impacted Kasia differently than her sisters.

I was in a zombie-like state of shock after being awakened to the horrific discovery. But that's no excuse. I feel embarrassed that as Emma's father, I did not perform the task left to Kasia. In fact, for twenty-five years I blacked out this fact from my memory. It wasn't until researching this book that I was told Kasia did the mouth-to-mouth. Even though I was in the room, I had totally forgotten this major detail of the night.

Kasia is to be commended for her leadership and heroics in doing whatever was asked of her that night. I wouldn't be the least surprised if she suffered post-traumatic stress disorder. PTSD is a mental health condition that's triggered by a terrifying event—either by experiencing it or witnessing it. A highly private person, Kasia has not told us if the event induced PTSD, so I'm hopeful that she does not suffer through symptoms like flashbacks, nightmares, and severe anxiety. She is now a successful communications professional in California and, more importantly, a loving wife, mother, sister, and daughter.

Psychologist and bereavement expert Stephen Fleming tells me PTSD in survivors is not uncommon following the death of a child, especially if it is a violent death. Emma's death was not caused by someone else, like a murderer or drunk driver, so hopefully PTSD is not haunting any of our daughters. (Some readers whose family have lost a child, may want to explore the PTSD possibility with a professional.)

There are also many general ways a child's death can affect siblings.

Surviving children experience intense emotions such as sadness, anger, guilt, and confusion following the death of a sibling. All our girls went through such feelings for varying periods of time.

After the funeral, burial, and family wake in our home, Kasia locked herself in her room for a week and only came out to eat or use the bathroom. Both Frances and I tried to engage Kasia, but she wanted her privacy and really only talked to Amanda. After the week-long seclusion, she was ready to return to school.

Amanda, who wasn't there when Emma's body was discovered, showed her artistic flair by writing poems and drawing pictures for Emma. Today, Amanda acknowledges that she relived

March 6, 1998, in her head every day for at least six months (her arrival later that afternoon on March 6 likely added to the anxiety) and she had a recurring dream where Emma was standing outside in the backyard but couldn't get back into the house. And, in the dream, when Amanda would try to bring Emma inside, Emma would disappear and the dream would end.

This poem, entitled "Emptiness," was written by Amanda when she was only fifteen years old, three years after Emma died:

I am empty inside, my love awakens everyday,
but fills me with pain and anger.
Every day I watch the outside world from the inside.
What is beyond the inside, I have not seen.
What is between us we cannot break, we are divided in two.
I can no longer see you, but in my dreams.
Whenever there is a cloud, you make it go away.
When I cry you are sad, when I smile you are happy.
You had never broken my heart, but now it is
torn because you have left my side.
In time, the space between us will break and I will
be in your world looking in instead of out.
I will wait for you if you wait for me, but I will
see you in my dreams until that day.
I wait for my heart to be unbroken.
It will have then been touched by an angel.

Little Melanie's reaction in the months after Emma's death was itself unique. Remember, she was only six years old when Emma died.

Melanie has vivid memories of the days around the time Emma died. She remembers the day before when Emma was coughing, then the day of the death a police officer reading her a story to shield her from the chaos in our home, going to school briefly that day, being in the funeral home and seeing her sister's body in the casket, the funeral service, and the wake in our home afterwards. But she has very few memories of things and events that happened over the next six months.

"Emma was wearing a green velvet pantsuit in the coffin, and I remember touching her and feeling how cold she was," says Melanie, now in her early thirties. "Then Dad's best friend, Dan [Bailey], took me out of the funeral home to a bookstore nearby."

One of her final memories of this time involves the family gathering in our home after the funeral. "Mom and her sisters were laughing, and I asked myself, 'Why are they laughing? This is a terrible time,'" Melanie says.

After that, it's as if someone zapped her memory bank and it's blank for the next six months. Playing pop psychologist, I'm guessing that "someone" was her subconscious trying to protect her. "I'm glad I don't have memories of my parents being so sad," says Melanie, now the mother of our first grandson, Archer.

Beyond the initial reactions, the loss of a sibling affects the entire family dynamic. Frances and I were both consumed by our own grief, and that may have left the girls feeling unsupported or neglected at times.

"It felt like the family was on autopilot in the dark," says Amanda, adding that both Frances and I suppressed our emotions in front of them to appear strong, or as strong as we could be.

That's an astute observation from Amanda. As I've already acknowledged, I donned a figurative cape and turned into Super Dad for the sake of the family, or so I thought. When it came to getting meals on the table, driving the kids to and from school and other activities, and anything else that needed to get done, that was up to me, Super Dad.

Maybe I should have expressed my emotions more to my girls during those initial weeks and months after Emma's passing. I don't know. I am, after all, not the sort of person who is good at hiding his emotions, but Emma's death was so transformational in my life that I tried.

"To me," Amanda says, "he was like a big bear hiding behind a small tree." Amanda and her artistic flair. She sure can paint a picture! She also believes I was "sweeping" things away, not grieving, by putting on the Super Dad act.

Another thing our girls had to cope with was an adjustment in routines, activities, and relationships within the family.

For example, Melanie says she became my "business buddy" who would tag along when I was working an open house or at the RE/MAX office. "My dad latched onto me because I was the youngest," Mel says. She remembers our many trips to Canada's Wonderland amusement park north of Toronto. Being the dad, I'd put restrictions on things like what she could eat or what arcade games she could play.

But when I took her a couple weeks after her seventh birthday—on July 30, 1998, and five months after Emma's death—I tried to make it special for Melanie. When we got to the park, I told her she could do whatever she wanted, no restrictions.

My heart melted as we were holding hands and leaving the park to go home. Melanie turned to me and said: "You're the best dad I have ever had." I told this story at her wedding more than twenty years later.

Curiously, and related to Melanie seemingly erasing her memory for the months after Emma died, today Mel admits she's not sure if she actually remembers saying that at the time or whether it's simply a story she has heard many times over.

"So much of my childhood was with Dad," Melanie says today. "I don't think he would have done that if Emma was there because he would have been sharing the time with me and Emma."

Labelling her younger years as "a happy childhood," losing her sister notwithstanding, Melanie says that by age nine or ten, she felt the need to go to friends' houses, in particular that of her best friend, Katie Rathgeber. Our home could be very dark at times, she says.

Our grieving and our pain over Emma had changed the way Melanie acted, she admits. "I always wanted to be away from home and with friends. I remember telling my mom that the family was not normal and always sad."

As I've noted, there is no road map when it comes to grieving the loss of a child. Frances and I did our best. Mistakes were made and it is my hope that candidly revealing them here may help other similarly suffering parents avoid a mistake or two along the way with their surviving children and/or spouse.

As with any parent who has lost a child, I could get paralyzed with fear, if I let it, when thoughts arose of possibly losing another child. I knew of other people who'd lost more than one child. There was Mrs. French who worked in the local post office. She and her husband lost all six of their children in a house fire while she was at work.

And I remembered an old TV commercial with two math nerds debating the percentage chances of an ostrich running down the street. One said there was a minuscule chance. Then an ostrich appeared running past them. Once he had witnessed the event, the math nerd modified his prediction to a 100 percent chance! That's how I felt: If one daughter could die, others could die, too. It's irrational but also believable once it's happened to you.

Anyway, through their teens I was "that dad" who always questioned their whereabouts, tried to vet their friendships and weed out bad apples, and generally hovered over them a little too much. I think I was protective, but my girls would say overprotective, especially as each moved into their high school years.

"He became so paranoid that something would happen to us after Emma died," Melanie says today. "I kind of turned into a hard teenager to deal with, and it became a self-fulfilling prophecy. I hated [the constant scrutiny] at the time, but I now understand he was worried and did those things out of love."

Then, in February 2006, when Melanie was fourteen, my fears came dangerously close to being realized. One of Mel's friends called and said we should come get her as she was asleep in a nearby park. When we arrived, we found it was more apt to say passed out than asleep—in the middle of winter—but we needn't dwell on the details during these teenage years.

Driving her home, Frances had Melanie on her lap in the backseat. All of a sudden, she said, "Rick, she's not breathing."

In a panic, I called 9-1-1 and the operator immediately dispatched help and told me to lay her flat on her back on our driveway and give her mouth-to-mouth. Yes, this time, I had my wits about me to do it! I got her breathing again and an ambulance whisked her off to hospital.

That was probably the scariest moment of my life versus Emma's death, which was the most horrific moment of my life. I've had a wonderful life in so many ways, but I have had some awful things happen, too.

Melanie was a challenging teenage girl, but she made it through high school, spread her wings in university, and today is a terrific, loving, and intelligent person whom I am so proud of, as I am of all my daughters, including Emma.

There's one more impact on our children that should be noted. Kasia and Amanda are fourteen months apart, and they were always best friends growing up. Melanie is six years younger than Amanda and often felt like a third wheel. When Emma arrived, Melanie always imagined their relationship would be like Kasia and Amanda's.

After Emma died, Mel says, "I remember thinking I wish Emma was here because I wanted the equivalent of what Kasia and Amanda had growing up. I don't feel that way now, but as a kid I did feel resentful."

We don't always know the feelings of our children at critical times. They don't always share, and often hide, their feelings. Not all of these points are applicable to my daughters, but they are worth noting for others.

- Siblings may feel guilty for not being able to prevent the death or for any conflicts they had with their sibling prior to their passing. They may also feel a sense of responsibility to carry on their sibling's legacy or to make up for their loss.
- The stress and trauma of losing a sibling can cause developmental regression in children, causing them to act younger than their age, become clingy, or experience difficulty sleeping or eating.
- Siblings may struggle to find their place in the family or in the world following the loss of their brother or sister. They may also question their own mortality and struggle with self-esteem and identity issues.
- Grief can affect a child's ability to focus on schoolwork, participate in extracurricular activities, or maintain

friendships. This can further exacerbate their sense of isolation and loss.

It's important for parents and caregivers to provide support and understanding for children who have lost a sibling. It's not easy, especially if you're a grieving parent, but it is essential. This can include creating a safe and open environment for communication, seeking counselling or therapy if needed, and allowing children to grieve and process their emotions in their own time and way.

There are no do-overs in life, and I did a lot of things correctly with Kasia, Amanda, and Melanie. If I could change anything about the years after Emma's death it would be trying *not* to act like a Super Dad. Instead, I would have focused on simply loving them, revealing my true self and not acting like someone different.

"My father," Amanda says, "immediately actioned the parent-protective role for the rest of us instead of openly grieving and relating to it all. And perhaps my mother just shut down. They both did their best."

Lesson learned: As the father, I felt I needed to be strong. But the girls simply wanted me to be me, and sometimes I wasn't.

It is not the will of your Father who is in Heaven
that one of these little ones perish.

— Matthew 18:14

Chapter 7

Spirituality

"It's God's will." I was told this by more than one person after Emma's death. Thankfully, not by too many people, and certainly not by our then-pastor, Dr. Jan Huntjens, or my good friends Don Gibson, a retired United Church minister, and Dan Bailey, a former United Church minister.

The other religious-based comment that would make me grit my teeth, put on a forced smile, and be polite was this beauty: "She's in a better place." That one really irked me, and still does.

No, you idiot, I would always think, but never say. A better place would be in my arms, at our dining room table, at nursery school, in her bed, walking down the aisle on her wedding day, still here living a life that was stolen from her—and all of us who love her.

William Sloane Coffin Jr., an American clergyman and long-time peace activist throughout the second half of the twentieth century, delivered a poignant eulogy for his son, Alex, in 1983, a mere ten days after the young man's car careened off a bridge during a winter storm and plunged into icy waters.

"For some reason, nothing so infuriates me as the incapacity of seemingly intelligent people to get it through their heads that God doesn't go around this world with his fingers on triggers, his fists around knives, his hands on steering wheels. God is dead set against all unnatural deaths," Coffin told his congregation at Riverside Church in New York City.

"My own consolation lies in knowing that it was not the will of God that Alex die; that when the waves closed over the sinking car, God's heart was the first of all our hearts to break."

Then he said something, including a quote from English poet Lord Byron about joy being taken from us, that really resonates:

"The reality of grief is the absence of God—'My God, my God, why hast thou forsaken me?' The reality of grief is the solitude of pain, the feeling that your heart is in pieces, your mind's a blank, that 'there is no joy the world can give like that it takes away,'" Dr. Coffin said.

I simply can't reconcile supposed religious statements with Emma's death. I've tried. I've read a lot. I've spoken extensively with religious people and ministers. I've spent years in grief therapy, and on many occasions, we've talked about God and Emma.

Actually, I remember being really angry with God. I had played by the rules: loving father, faithful husband, dutiful churchgoer, and someone who always put family first.

And then God let me down by taking this beautiful child away from her family. It broke Frances's heart, and I was not sure, in the beginning, that she would be able to recover and love the rest of us, let alone any future grandchildren. Thankfully, my fears were unfounded and any anger in my heart toward God subsided.

Still, I can find no clear answer why she was taken from us. Religion and Emma's death simply don't go together in my mind. And that is one reason why, over the years, I have drifted from organized religion and moved more into the realm of spirituality. Emma's death challenged my faith and beliefs about the world as well as my sense of purpose and meaning.

Her death changed my life irrevocably. For a very long time, I felt as if everything I focused on was important and meaningful (my career, making money, buying rental properties). Then, suddenly, all that became hollow and insignificant. To this day, I find myself questioning so many long-held beliefs. I don't fully understand why she died or what any of it means.

I do believe in God, or some supreme being, but I question its role in my life. I used to be a regular churchgoer, but not anymore. I remember looking at people in the pews, praying diligently on Sunday and possibly doing less than Christian things at other times during the week.

It's kind of like people who say they support Ukraine in that unjust war that began with Russia's invasion in February 2022. These people fly blue and yellow Ukrainian flags and pray for a peaceful resolution and an end to the bloodshed.

But beyond that, what are they doing? Are they opening their homes temporarily to any of the 200,000 Ukrainian war refugees who've landed in Canada? Are they donating food, money, and clothing or helping refugees find permanent places to live in Canada? I hope so, but I fear most do little more than fly flags. I don't mean to be preachy, but talk is cheap. And sometimes organized religion feels too much like talk and not enough about action to help the less fortunate.

Of course, there are many good people who attend churches, mosques, synagogues, and temples. I've had the honour of working alongside many terrific people as we were finding apartments and furnishing them for refugees coming to the Toronto area. Many of them are churchgoers.

I like action and simple good deeds over abstract concepts. Maybe that's one thing that has come from the loss of Emma? It's chased me from the pews and out into the world to try to live life more under the Christian ideal of doing unto others.

Some of these simple acts include helping friends by driving them to medical appointments, checking in on people who are struggling, running errands, dropping off a meal, or simply keeping people company when they're blue or unhappy. Simple day-to-day things. I'm definitely not perfect, but the loss of Emma has made me try to do my best every day. Obviously, there are many days when I fall short of my goal. But I try.

Natalie Kotyck, the former RE/MAX agent and good friend I've walked with for twenty-five years, remembers one occasion that I had long forgotten. She says, "I remember a few years ago, after I had a knee replacement, the doctor told me my red-blood-cell count was low and that I needed more iron in my diet. I told Rick this and the next thing I know he's at my door with a meal of calf's liver from ViBo restaurant. He does things like that."

Dan Bailey tells the story about recovering from prostate surgery in 2007. He mentioned wanting to visit his elderly parents in Fergus, Ontario, an hour and a half away. He couldn't drive, so I took him. No big deal.

"He's always asking 'how can I help?' That's Rick," Dan says.

I like to think I've evolved and don't need to go to church. I'd rather actively help friends and do community work to help others.

While organized religion has taken a backseat, I most definitely believe there is some powerful force in the universe. I do have a complicated relationship with religion. In 2023, Frances and I visited Cartagena, Colombia, for a wedding and extended our stay as part of our vacation.

While I was out walking alone, music from a church drew me inside. There was a Catholic mass going on and people were receiving sacraments. I sat down in a pew and prayed for Emma. I felt something that day—a force of some sort. I began crying silently and left the church to continue my solitary walk through old Cartagena, still sniffling much of the walk.

And, as I've alluded to, there have just been too many unexplainable coincidences at play in Emma's story that point to something or someone being up there.

I've mentioned our first grandchild being born on November 17, 2019, which would have been Emma's twenty-fourth birthday. I've also pointed out the significance of the Lillian Rose and little Natalie Demeter graves so close to Emma's and the sensation I sometimes get within that triangle at the cemetery.

Indeed, my friend Don Gibson drove me to the cemetery the day Emma died because we didn't own a family plot, or any plot. The woman at the cemetery office said she had several sites available. Don drove Frances and me to look at the plots, and at the second one, I immediately said, "this is the one."

My grandparents and other relatives were in the adjacent section, and I felt it would be good to be near them. The location later proved to be special, and I think Emma guided me on the choice.

But there have been many more puzzling occurrences, including these:

The stained glass window

Many years ago, and as a way to honour Emma, I ordered a stained glass window to be made and installed at Kingsway-Lambton United Church. It's a beautiful and colourful depiction of peace and tranquility with three children and a dove in a garden filled with pansies. At the bottom it reads: "Thank you for the Love, Laughter, Joy and Hugs. A gift from the Emma Johnston Memorial Fund. Dedicated November 17, 2013."

That date was Emma's eighteenth birthday. Reverend Hugh Reid, Kingsway-Lambton's pastor from 2001 to 2023, had selected this date without knowing it was Emma's birthday.

The first date

All four of my daughters adored Gabriela Mendl, who was one of their youngest caregivers and worked for us from age fifteen until going off to university the autumn before Emma died. Kasia, Amanda, and Melanie loved playing a game called "beauty salon" with Gaby. They would do her hair and makeup real fancy as only young girls can do. As Emma got older, she would watch, giggle, and even laugh at how they'd "transform" Gaby.

Gaby's parents were clients of mine who became friends, as did Gaby. She and her husband, Mark, were at Kasia and Amanda's weddings, but were away when Melanie married.

As I mentioned previously, Gaby and Mark's first date was the evening of March 6, 1998, the day Emma passed.

That evening, I phoned Gaby's parents to give them the bad news. Gaby was out for dinner at La Marche restaurant and then was going to a movie with Mark. Her parents went to bed and decided to tell her the news the next morning.

"I was surprised how much it affected me," Gaby says today. "Three weeks after the funeral, I broke down for some reason in a chemistry lab [while studying human biology at the University of Toronto]. Who knows what triggered it, and it happened more than once."

She and Mark have two sons, and they have been happily married almost twenty-five years. "If I'd ever had a girl, her middle name would have been Emma," Gaby says. Her relationship with Mark began the day we lost Emma.

The last baptism

After almost fifteen years in the ministry with the United Church of Canada, Dan Bailey decided to become a teacher in early 1996, which he naturally excelled at for more than twenty years.

He will always remember, and cherish, that fact that Emma was the last child he baptized.

The lost child

The summer before Emma died, all six of us went for an outing to the idyllic village of Kleinburg, in the city of Vaughan and about an hour north of our Etobicoke home. Kleinburg is most famous as home to the McMichael Canadian Art Collection, an art gallery with a focus on the Group of Seven. But there are also many lovely shops and restaurants in the village. It was one of our favourite spots for family day trips.

In the summer of 1999, a year after Emma passed, Frances and I screwed up the courage to return to Kleinburg. On that beautiful sunny day, both Frances and I commented that it brought back fond memories of walking around the village with Emma in her stroller and the other girls in tow.

We walked around Kleinburg and, just like when Emma was with us, we had brunch at Mr. McGregor's House, a delightful restaurant in the village. This time, Melanie was the only girl with us. We sat in the garden under a huge oak tree and ate.

There was a harpist playing beautiful, melodic, memory-inducing music. When we finished eating, I approached the harpist and complimented her. She thanked me and said she had a CD for sale, which I purchased. It was entitled *The Lost Child*. Both Frances and I agreed it was another message from Emma.

The not lost child

In the spring of 1998, about two months after Emma died, I needed a pick-me-up. I went shopping at Plant World on Eglinton Avenue in Etobicoke. Walking around and looking at the various plants, I came upon purple and yellow pansies, Lillian Rose's favourite flower, which Emma also liked.

Figuring I'd plant these annuals in our garden, I put some in my cart. Just then, a beautiful blue-eyed little girl approached and was looking at the pansies, too.

"Hello," I said.

She smiled and just as we were about to strike up a little conversation, I heard her mother in the other aisle say: "Come along, Emma." She waved goodbye.

Unexplainable messages

Both Frances and I believe Emma has sent us messages that we, as mere mortals, cannot fully understand in this realm. They've come to us consciously and in our sleep. We believe these messages are manifested from some sort of spiritual force or unexplainable energy in the universe.

After the death of a child some parents become very religious to help them cope. And that's okay. As the title of the John Lennon song says, "Whatever Gets You Thru the Night." Others jettison God and religion.

I'm somewhere in the middle. At first, I blamed God. I no longer do. And I do believe in a Higher Force. Some day, I believe, I will fully understand why she was taken, but I will likely not find answers in this life. For any bereaved parent who blames God, or who has lost faith, I would urge you to Google William Sloane Coffin's eulogy for his son and read it, with a box of tissues close by.

Photographs

Memorial window for Emma's 18th birthday, dedicated November 17, 2013

Family picture, Fall 1997

Family picture, October 2023

Emma's sisters, 2023

*Empathy is thin gruel compared
to the marrow of experience.*

— J. R. MOEHRINGER, AUTHOR

Chapter 8

Hugs, Casseroles, and What Not to Say

The day after Emma died, my friend and neighbour Janna Adair arrived at our door with lots of food for the family and treats for the girls, Kasia, Amanda, and Melanie. She also gave me a much-needed hug. Tears flowed down our cheeks.

Janna then noticed a full laundry basket of clothes just out of the dryer on a table. She marched us both into the kitchen and sat us down while she folded laundry and I tried to find words. Sometimes we just sat in silence as she folded shirts and sheets.

"I've always believed that in the mundane, small things of everyday life, not only do we find joy, but I think we also find compassion in sorrow," Janna says.

The previous morning, she knew something was amiss during her daily early morning walk at 6:30 a.m. when she saw a police car at our house. Being a teacher at our girls' public school, she heard the news later that morning from Melanie's teacher. Janna immediately started thinking about what she could do to help.

Some people, like Janna, instinctively get it. Others, not so much.

This chapter is certainly not meant to embarrass or ridicule anyone. Its intent is to shed some light on the mental state of bereaved parents and help well-meaning friends and family be sensitive and mindful of their feelings.

Let's face it, it can be awkward to console people who've lost someone precious, especially if it's a death "out of time," as is the case with a child. Sometimes the right words don't come, or sometimes what is thought to be the right words are not.

When in doubt, use the KISS principle: Keep It Simple, Stupid! A simple "I'm sorry" or "sorry for your loss" goes a lot further than getting tongue-tied trying to come up with the right words.

And here's a tip that is really important: never shy away from using the deceased child's name. Use the name as often as possible. I know I had this visceral need to hear the word "Emma." I still love hearing it, all these years later. The more I hear it, the more she and her memory stay alive in my heart. No parent wants their deceased child washed away like footprints on the beach.

As co-authors Stephen Fleming and Jennifer Buckle found after interviewing dozens and dozens of bereaved parents for their book *Parenting After the Death of a Child*, talking about their lost child is a need in every parent.

"Uniformly, parents find comfort and solace when friends and family members have the courage to engage them in conversations about their child," they report.

And don't only use the child's name. Tell bereaved parents why their child was important. Or, as Nobel laureate Toni

Morrison expressed succinctly after the death of her forty-five-year-old son, Slade, to pancreatic cancer in 2010:

"People speak to me about my son—'I'm so sorry for you'—but no one says, 'I loved him so much,'" says Morrison, expressing a sentiment felt by so many bereaved parents.

If you knew the child, especially if you had a relationship, tell his or her parents what made the child so special. If you didn't know the child, simple condolences and sympathy still go a long way.

And when it comes to offers of help or assistance, they're terrific gestures but don't expect bereaved parents to take you up on it by calling and asking for the support you offered. It doesn't work that way. "Bereaved parents are not going to reach out," Dr. Fleming says.

Doing something specific is always better than an open-ended general offer. Checking in with phone calls and texts are fine, but don't expect instant replies or any reply. Nothing beats knocking on the door with a casserole and a hug or asking a bereaved parent to join you for a walk or lunch, as so many friends did for me.

In the previous chapter on spirituality, I mentioned a couple things related to religion that should never be said, but there are more, many more—religious and otherwise—that should be avoided.

When talking to bereaved parents, here are some things you should never say to them:

TIME HEALS ALL WOUNDS. Grief is a complex and ongoing process, and it's not something that can be easily "fixed" or "healed" with time. That's why "let time heal your wounds" is a well-intentioned piece of assistance that might be the absolute worst advice for anyone trying to live and find meaning after the emotional pain of losing a child.

I KNOW HOW YOU FEEL. No, you don't! And comparing the death of a child to losing a parent or sibling who've lived a full life can be very insulting. Besides, everyone experiences grief differently, and even if you yourself have also lost a child, your experience may be very different. But if you've never lost a child, never say you know how they feel.

AT LEAST YOU HAVE OTHER CHILDREN. The loss of a child is a unique and irreplaceable loss, and the presence of other children does not diminish that pain. As I've said, I will always be a father of four, not three. Indeed, mentioning other children can actually stir up negative thoughts in bereaved parents. "If it happened to one, it could happen to another or all my children," a parent might think after such a comment from a friend. Although not exactly rational, this thought has crossed my mind many times.

Along these lines, my friends George and Kata Demeter, who lost their daughter Natalie, received a real punch to the gut from an oblivious person. Natalie was their only child, and shortly after her passing George's work in commercial real estate took them to Calgary, where most neighbours didn't know their story.

At a party, children were being kids and acting rambunctious. Amid the noise and chaos, one mother turned to them and said, "You're lucky you don't have children. They can be such hard work."

Despite it being a rather innocent comment to most, the words stung and have stuck with George and Kata for more than forty years! We never know other people's stories.

IT WAS GOD'S PLAN. This is a derivative of "God's will" or "she's in a better place" or "she's a real angel now." While some people may find comfort in their religious beliefs, it's important to remember that not everyone shares the same beliefs, and statements like this can be hurtful or dismissive. Besides, as stated earlier, clergyman William Sloane Coffin eloquently said God is not up there looking to take lives. Bad things happen all the time.

AVOID SCRIPTURE. As above, not everyone shares the same faith or wants to hear words from the Bible when they are likely still angry at God—and obviously still confused and in a daze. "Like God, Scripture is not around for anyone's protection, just for everyone's unending support," Coffin said. People who wish for it will find the Scripture they need. You don't need to supply it.

YOU SHOULD BE OVER IT BY NOW. Some people may say it outright, others infer it. But grief has no timeline. Once again, here are the important words from Dr. Fleming: "Your head tells time, not your heart." Everyone processes their emotions differently. It's important to allow bereaved parents to grieve at their own pace without judgment or pressure.

IT'S TIME TO MOVE ON. This is the sibling statement to "you should be over it by now." Grief is a journey, and it's not something that can be rushed or forced. Encouraging someone to "move on" can feel dismissive of their pain. And besides, what gives the "consoler" the right to judge another person and their individual grieving process?

Grief is a complicated process, and out-of-time deaths add another complex layer, especially for parents, but also for siblings, grandparents, and other close relatives. We should always keep in mind that grieving is universal, but everybody grieves differently.

And even if one says the wrong thing, that person shouldn't feel too bad. Even so-called professionals get it wrong, as Frances's first grief counsellor did.

"At my first session, she said I was blaming God and that I should burn all of Emma's things," Frances says. "She was crazy and definitely the wrong therapist for me."

After the second session, Frances never went back and found a different counsellor, who really helped over the years.

Through social media, I stumbled upon "The 10 Commandments of Loving Parents Who Lost a Child." The commandments were written by an American Catholic priest and grief counsellor named Father John Stabeno. The entire document is readily available via an Internet search, but I'll list the highlights here:

1. Fasten your seatbelts, it is going to be a bumpy ride! Expect the unexpected. Just be yourself.

2. Don't expect the person they were before the death of their child to come back. What used to matter before doesn't as much.

3. Don't expect sympathy for trivial stuff . . . and to them, it is all trivial stuff!

4. Don't feel bad if they don't call or hang out like they used to.

5. Expect the truth out of their mouths even if it appears cold and callous—there are zero effs given and no sugar coating!

6. Don't be afraid to mention their kids to them. They like when people talk about their children.

7. We cannot compare any of our losses to their loss (please don't say you understand if you have not lost a child). We have thankfully not walked in their shoes—so let's not pretend to.

8. Let them be where they are in their grief process and not where we think they should be at a given time.

9. Don't be deceived by appearances. They may look good on the outside and have their mask on that they use when they walk out of the house.

10. Be loyal and you will get loyalty back. Their circle of family and friends gets smaller from day one, and if you are lucky to remain in it, then you will then learn the meaning of true love at any cost.

Despite these ten commandments and other advice, friendships will change. Since the bereaved parent has changed so much inside, relationships are bound to change. Some people who were really close will drift off; other friends whom the bereaved didn't view as close before will form friendships that tighten and flourish. There are many reasons for this, from the "fear factor" of emotional discussions becoming awkward to bereaved persons being more discerning and avoiding what they consider trivial friendships.

I've lived it, and I can offer this advice on interacting with a bereaved parent, especially when the loss is still new and raw. In a nutshell, it's best to offer condolences and support without trying to offer solutions or your ideas on how to minimize their loss. A simple "I'm here for you" or "I'm so sorry for your loss" can go a long way in showing compassion and understanding.

Hugs are also important. Understand the power of simply being there in silence with your bereaved friend or family member. And never underestimate the impact of bringing a casserole or any type of comfort food, especially when there are other children to feed!

Always keep in mind that bereaved parenting is never about getting over it, or accepting it, or moving on with life, or any sort of resolution. It's about regeneration and a new reality that includes so much pain and a broken heart. It's about never getting over the loss but picking up the pieces after devastation and regenerating a new life with purpose.

The same boiling water that softens
the potato hardens the egg.

— ANTHONY J. JAMES,
INDIE FILM DIRECTOR

Chapter 9

Good Grief

Life tosses formidable challenges at all of us. There's no escaping bad things from happening. But it's not the boiling water—or the circumstances and events thrown at us in life—it's what we're made of, how we react, and whether we harden or soften.

As Forrest Gump said, life is like a box of chocolates and you never know what you're going to get. From experience, I can say life is a lot easier when we pull a chocolate from the box we like instead of being forced to eat one we'd prefer to spit out.

Unequivocally, Emma's death was the worst thing to happen to me. But I've now lived a lot longer and understand I've been blessed with a loving wife, children and grandchildren, fairly good health over my seventy years, and a career I love that has been financially rewarding.

Emma's death changed me from the inside out. I look similar (except maybe for the grey hair now), but I am most certainly different. I can't even remember what I was like before. My whole psyche has undergone a huge change.

It makes sense, though. After losing Emma, I wouldn't want to be the same person I was. I've examined my life, and my family is the most important thing, followed by meaningful friendships. Material things don't mean the same anymore. There's a reason why I stopped buying and selling rental properties for more than a decade after Emma died. Instead, I focused on trips and experiences with loved ones—not renovations and resale properties.

It is difficult for me to say this, but maybe some good—the proverbial silver lining—did come from the storm clouds in my life after Emma's death. It has taken many years and tears to reach this conclusion, but her death eventually led me to what I call "good grief": my broken heart seemed to grow in many ways, especially when it comes to understanding and identifying pain in others.

I think this has made me a better, more caring person. I've learned to let go of trivial things. I've tried to laugh a little harder, breathe a little deeper, and love a little stronger.

For several years after Emma's death, I was living a lie. I wore the metaphorical mask of Super Dad to keep my family, my marriage, and my life afloat. As a father, with both a wife and three living daughters depending on me, I felt that I must cope and be strong for the sake of the family. I worked harder than ever, both to provide for my family and to keep my mind as busy as possible in a rather futile effort to keep thoughts of Emma at bay, at least during the workday.

Like so many others, and because grief is so painful, my early reactions were to avoid situations or people that reminded me of losing Emma. I tended to avoid interaction with young children because just seeing their smiling faces and their joie de vivre triggered feelings of sadness and loss.

And the trouble with avoidance is it tends to spread. I then started to avoid the children's parents and families. Then I avoided people who said or did things that stirred up aching memories. It's why I never liked group therapy or grieving groups where you would be asked to participate and share. If I wasn't in the correct head space, I just wanted privacy and to keep my feelings about what happened to myself. I'm sure other bereaved parents have felt the same way.

Along these lines, I am thankful to several clergy who intrinsically knew this about me. If I was in the proper head space, I'd talk to them, and they always listened and helped. People like Reverend Jan Huntjens, a kind man who seemed to genuinely feel the injustice of losing a child, former minister Dan Bailey, my friend Don Gibson, a minister at a nearby church at the time who was my source for Bible passages about love, and David Windsor, a pastoral care minister at Kingsway-Lambton United Church. I trust they all know how helpful they were to me in the first few years and continue to be today.

Early on, my public façade masked private despair for many, many months. I was an emotional basket case. I had this idea that it didn't seem right to grieve publicly. I appeared okay to most people, but my closest friends and family knew I was little more than flotsam and jetsam bouncing about in rough internal waters. I am forever grateful for these people who understood how much I needed them, even if it meant spending time with me in silence or in fits of weeping.

Eventually, I emerged from this debilitating grief and anguish. And, coincidentally or not, it was around this time that many of my good friends needed me in their own grief or other challenging times. If I was in a stable spot mentally, I'd do my best to help.

I must admit to sometimes experiencing "grief spikes"—the all-encompassing and mentality debilitating grief that comes flooding back, as it did in the early days after Emma's death—that prevented me from helping as much as I would have liked. As time marched on, grief spikes would hit me less frequently, but their intensity would always be overwhelming.

Some say grief eases with time. If you picture a graph, it has the "grief and sadness level" vertically running up the left and "time since death"' horizontally across the bottom. One continuous line begins at the top on the left at the time of loss and runs lower and lower down to the bottom right when the grief is effectively gone.

But that's not my experience. My grief journey continues. There's always something about Emma in the background. And, thankfully, the emotional grief spikes are broken up now with daily, weekly, sometimes even monthly, spaces between them.

Or, as grief expert Dr. Fleming explains, "Grief is not short term and finite. The time dimension doesn't matter." The head tells time, not the heart . . .

Given all this, how can there be hidden benefits of grief? Grief is horrible. It makes us want to curl into a ball and pull the covers over our heads. It is painful, raw, confusing, and can last forever. I'm still grieving Emma twenty-five years later.

So, how can we find any benefits in that? As they say, grief is the price we pay for love. It took me a long time to fully understand that. Allow me to make my case for "good grief."

My grief journey has taught me the following: acceptance of things I can't change, a better appreciation for life and to make the most of every day, a better understanding of myself and my strengths, confidence that I can cope with anything life throws at me, and a clearer understanding of others—especially those in the throes of grief. In a nutshell, to value what's truly important in life and to let go of trivial matters.

Neuroscientist Mary-Frances O'Connor studies grief and the brain. In her latest book, *The Grieving Brain*, she uses science to explain why grieving is a heart-wrenching and painful problem for the brain to solve.

"For the brain, your loved one is simultaneously gone and also everlasting, and you are walking through two worlds at the same time. You are navigating your life despite the fact that they have been stolen from you, a premise that makes no sense, and that is both confusing and upsetting," writes O'Connor, an associate professor of psychology at the University of Arizona.

Although few of us realize it at the time, O'Connor says going through the grieving process makes us stronger personalities and better able to cope with challenges.

Only one year after Emma's death, a former colleague of mine from my days working in government died of a heart attack at his home in our Etobicoke neighbourhood. Bill Javorski was only forty-eight years old. He and his wife, Linda, were dear friends of ours. Bill was truly in love with Linda. I've never met a man who always, and I mean always, talked so proudly and glowingly about his wife.

"Few people," I told Linda, "find someone in life who is so devotedly in love with them. Bill was that for you."

I understood that comment meant a lot to her in her darkest hours. Would I have said it without being in the midst of my own grief journey? Had my personality gotten stronger and helped me cope with challenges, as Dr. O'Connor stated above? I don't know.

It's not like grief was a new experience for me. My father died when I was only seventeen years old and my sister, Brenda, died three weeks before Emma, but their deaths did not have the impact on my life that Emma's did. Perhaps, the silver lining of grief brought on by Emma is what brought those words to my mouth that comforted Linda. Who knows?

As the great Russian writer and philosopher Dostoevsky said, "It is always so, when we are unhappy we feel more strongly the unhappiness of others; our feeling is not shattered, but becomes concentrated." So, maybe Emma did help me help my friend Linda in her time of pain.

I've lost several other friends and family since Bill passed, including Rosamund Foster (pancreatic cancer in 2003), Frances's brother Michael Klimowski (heart attack at home at age fifty in 2013), close friend Blair Baxter (heart attack at Pearson International Airport in 2021 while waiting to fly south on vacation), and church friend Steve Prime (died at age sixty-two in June 2018). In each case, I made an effort to console their grieving partners with visits, food, and hugs.

I've also done my best to help friends with cancer by driving them to medical appointments or to visit their parents when they couldn't drive. Once, I even took a friend to her cottage to relax and get a break from the chemotherapy for a few days.

In each case, I'd like to think my grief journey played a role by increasing my capacity for empathy and understanding. For me, personally, I think this is part of Emma's legacy: she helped make her dad a better, more helpful person. In the next chapter, I will get into more detail about her overall legacy.

From my personal perspective, I must address a controversial issue involving grief and psychiatry. Prolonged Grief Disorder (PGD) can occur when someone close to the bereaved has died within at least six months for children and within twelve months for adults.

The grief is so intense that it debilitates people, impacts their ability to work and function socially, and it can bring on suicidal thoughts. PGD is estimated to affect about 4–7 percent of bereaved people in the general population, with higher rates when the death is sudden, unexpected, or violent, and when a young person dies.

In 2022, the fifth edition of the *Diagnostic and Statistical Manual of Mental Disorders*—known better as DSM-5 or "psychiatry's Bible"—was amended to classify PGD as a form of mental illness. In other words, the official psychiatric community is saying intense grief is not a normal part of the human experience and it is like depression and other forms of mental illnesses. Not all the experts agree with that assessment.

PGD has been studied since the 1990s and was known as "complicated grief" before the formal DSM-5 designation. It has been a recognized diagnosis by the World Health Organization since 2018.

Proponents of the PGD mental illness designation say these severely grieving people need tailored treatment, including drug therapy, to help them successfully carry on with life.

Opponents of it say grieving is a normal part of the human experience and the designation implies it is not normal. I tend to agree that putting a time frame on grieving is wrong. I didn't wake up after a year and magically rub my hands, kiss my wife and kids, and declare, "I'm all better and over Emma now."

I'm not over Emma. I never want to be over Emma.

Opponents also fear the designation will turn grief into a "growth market" for Big Pharma and doctors will over-prescribe and over-medicate patients in grief. For the record, in the early days I took prescribed medication to help me sleep, but my grief journey has never pushed me to take anti-depressants. I had witnessed what prescription drugs did to my sister and how they led to her demise. With my therapist, Dr. Canella, my treatment was all about talk therapy.

Of course, for someone who still grieves his daughter twenty-five years later, some may suspect I have PGD. I've sometimes wondered that, too.

Here are the symptoms identified by the American Psychiatric Association in 2022. If you experience three or more, a PGD diagnosis can be made:

- Identity disruption (such as feeling as though part of oneself has died).
- Marked sense of disbelief about the death.
- Avoidance of reminders that the person is dead.
- Intense emotional pain (such as anger, bitterness, sorrow) related to the death.
- Difficulty with reintegration (such as problems engaging with friends, pursuing interests, planning for the future).
- Emotional numbness (absence or marked reduction of emotional experience).
- Feeling that life is meaningless.
- Intense loneliness (feeling alone or detached from others).

By reading this book, one could identify a number of these symptoms in me and mentioned in these pages. The last three are the only ones that I can truthfully say are most definitely not me.

But here's the rub: just because I've experienced five of these eight symptoms at one time or another—sometimes fifteen years after Emma's death—doesn't make me feel I am "suffering" from PGD.

Indeed, during the worst days, where I describe myself in a near-catatonic state of grief, I was functioning—working and keeping the household running. And this occurred long after the one-year period since Emma's death.

I remember going to see my family doctor for an annual checkup a couple years after Emma's passing. Dr. E. H. Schweihofer was my GP for more than thirty years, and I really cared for him. Now retired, Dr. Schweihofer always took the time to listen, and he was a very good diagnostic doctor.

Anyway, at this annual checkup, I told him I thought I was depressed. He looked me in the eye and said, "Well, you have every right to be." Then he spent extra time just talking to me about grief, which was very comforting.

If a PGD diagnosis helps a bereaved person to deal with their grief, I'm all for it. It's just not for me.

Instead of prescription drugs, I prefer to hold onto the positive effects of "good grief," and all the related tools, to help me cope, while at the same time keeping my relationship with Emma alive in my heart.

Section Three

Regeneration

*A person will be just about as happy
as they make up their minds to be.*

— ABRAHAM LINCOLN

Chapter 10

Legacy

On Canada Day 2023, I delivered a cheque from the Emma Johnston Memorial Fund to a Brampton apartment where a five-year-old boy named Mark lives with his mother Maria. They are Ukrainian refugees from the bloody war that Russian dictator Vladimir Putin has waged against an independent country and its civilians.

Maria answered the door with her son by her side. The mom was friendly, and the boy was confident, speaking good English. Mark engaged with me and shared that he had just finished senior kindergarten and was excited to be going into grade 1.

It was a brief visit, but I couldn't help but think: What atrocities has this little boy witnessed? Will he ever see his father again? What deep-seated psychological scars, if any, will he battle going forward?

So, what is Mark's connection to the Emma Johnston Memorial Fund? Mark had asked his mom if he could go to a traditional Canadian summer camp in the woods with a bunch of his new friends from school. Obviously, she couldn't afford to send him to camp. Through other Ukrainian refugees, she heard about Emma's fund and applied for financial assistance.

At that Brampton apartment, and after handing Maria the cheque to pay for Mark's summer camp adventure, I took out a family picture from my wallet. The photograph was from just months before Emma's passing. I pointed to Emma in the picture and talked a little bit about her. It was a lovely exchange, and I think Emma was proud to help Mark go to camp.

Emma was physically with us less than thirty months—809 days, to be precise—and she taught us all so much, in particular how to give and receive unconditional love. She brought so much joy to all our lives and instilled in me and the family some sort of magical strength that kept us going immediately after, and that keeps me going today.

After her death, I wanted to put some of that goodness that we lost back into the world. My friend Judy Guthrie, a real estate agent I'd come to know through open houses and other industry events, came up with the idea for the Emma Johnston Memorial Fund. Judy was the driving force behind raising an initial $10,000 from real estate agents. Family, friends, and churchgoers have also made generous contributions.

The fund is run and administered through Kingsway-Lambton United Church. Its main focus is to help financially strapped people with their education. We review applications, interview the applicants with the most compelling stories, and give what we can to those most in need. During the first years after its inception, someone from the church would deliver cheques to the recipients. It was just too emotionally difficult for me at the time.

Over the last decade or so, I have taken on the role of delivering the cheques and meeting the recipients. I like to think of the money as a helping "hand up," not a "hand out." And I can honestly say that meeting the people and telling them about Emma and what her life meant to us brings me so much pleasure.

I remember one year talking to a young woman who wanted to be a nurse, but she needed help to pay for adult education courses. Her application said she was married, so I asked if her husband could help her reach her dream, too.

"He can't," she said. "He's in prison."

Like a slap to the side of my head, it hit me: despite all the challenges and pain in my life, I still have it pretty darn good. We should all remember that not everyone lives like us. Emma and her fund taught me this lesson. It warms me to think that the Emma Johnston Memorial Fund helped in a small way for this woman to become a valuable frontline worker in our community today.

At the outset, Emma's fund was geared to helping people roughly the age Emma would have been had she lived. In the early years, it was for young children, then teens, then young adults.

As stated earlier, I've always pictured Emma at various stages of life: graduating grade school, then high school, and ultimately university. Starting her career, getting married, having children. All the so-called normal things in life. On the other hand, Frances can't imagine Emma in various stages of life. Emma is frozen in Frances's psyche as a little, cuddly two-and-a-half-year-old girl.

Neither parent's imagination is right or wrong, good or bad—just different.

And it explains why the Emma fund has been flexible in helping all sorts of different people over the years. After Putin's unjust invasion of Ukraine in February 2022, we shifted the focus to help refugee children. Besides little Mark going to summer camp, the fund has paid for another refugee boy's soccer season and a little girl's dance lessons that she desperately wanted but were not affordable for her mother.

As a pastor decades ago, and later as a teacher, Dan Bailey is a person familiar with deaths of young people and their impact on others. Indeed, there was one dreadful five-year period when six of Dan's students (or former students) died: two suicides, one from a fentanyl overdose, one from a car accident, and two in a house fire on Christmas Eve. From these experiences, Dan learned the importance of keeping the children's memory alive.

Asked about the Emma fund, Dan says, "Rick feels a responsibility to keep this fund going because it helps him keep the memories of Emma and her life alive in his heart and elsewhere."

Don Gibson, a retired pastor who presided over at least one child funeral per year for forty years, said bereaved parents ultimately benefit when they move into a "mission stage" after the death of their child.

"Some come to it earlier than others, some never do," Don says. "The ones who do well all seem to find a mission or a purpose."

I'm proud of my daughter, and I'm proud of the Emma fund. It's not huge and grandiose like some funds in memory of celebrities and rich people. Its goal is to serve those in our community, not all around the country or the world. Emma wasn't famous or anything, so the fund seems to fit snugly and comfortably like an old sweater. I believe she approves.

It's also another way for me and my family to help maintain a relationship with Emma—by relocating, not relinquishing, her from our memories and life. (When I'm gone, Emma's sister Amanda will take over as head of the fund.)

I believe all bereaved parents—not just me and Frances—are constantly seeking new ways to continue the relationship with their deceased child. Detachment is a dirty word for those in the fraternity of the unthinkable. The Emma fund helps maintain a deep and continuing connection between me and my daughter, all while helping others in our community.

As long as there's money in the Emma fund, it will continue to help others, and I think Emma would really love that.

While the fund is a large part of Emma's legacy, it is by no means the only way we honour her. The beautiful stained glass window in her name at Kingsway-Lambton United Church is another, as is a memorial bench I had built and installed outside the church's nursery, where weary parents in need of a breather could sit and rest! (Fun fact: there were two symbols Emma would immediately recognize and talk about. One was the steeple at Kingsway-Lambton United Church and the other was McDonald's golden arches: a place of worship and the temple of fast food. The juxtaposition makes me smile.)

To honour her legacy, we've also done personal things like place candles, say prayers, and release helium balloons at her gravesite on her birthday, November 17, and on March 6, the day she passed. Over the first few years, Kasia, Amanda, and Melanie would put special written messages to Emma in helium balloons and release them into the air at the cemetery while each held a candle and said a prayer for their sister.

Now, on these special dates, it is me and Frances going to the gravesite and lighting five candles to represent those in her immediate family who miss but will never forget her. Each November 17 and March 6 there are still a flurry of family text messages about Emma, which I think are important for all of us.

Big or small, doing things to further a loved one's legacy is healthy for all, especially for the bereaved parents. Legacy echoes a life lived—an important life that taught us many things. In our case, with Emma, what reverberates in her legacy is the importance of unconditional love and joy. For someone who was in this world for little more than eight hundred days, Emma left us quite a gift.

While creating a legacy can never replace the loss, it can provide comfort and a sense of purpose, like our charitable fund has done for me. Here are some other ideas on how to create a lasting legacy for a deceased child:

- Scholarship fund. Establish a scholarship fund in your child's name to support other children in pursuing their education.

- Artistic expression. Encourage artistic endeavours that celebrate your child's life. The arts can be so effective in unlocking life's secrets. As the saying goes, "Art is life." This could involve creating art, music, or literature inspired by the deceased loved one's memory.

- Community service. Do volunteer work—like helping at a food bank—in your child's memory. This can help you channel grief into positive actions that benefit others.

- Memorial garden or place of contemplation. In honour of your child, establish a memorial garden or park for reflection and meditation or simply as a beautiful space where people can hang out and enjoy themselves.

- Awareness campaign. Start an awareness campaign related to a cause or issue that is important to you and your child. This can help raise awareness and funds for that cause. A poignant and important example of this is Mothers Against Drunk Driving. MADD was founded in 1980 by Candice Lightner, a mother in California whose daughter was killed by an impaired motorist. The international non-profit organization aims to stop drunk driving and support those who are affected by it.

➤ Book or documentary. Consider writing a book or creating a documentary about your child's life and the impact they had on your family and community. I know this book project has been quite an eye-opener for me and my family. I'd been thinking about it for more than ten years, and when I first proposed the idea, the family was against it, saying that it would merely open old wounds. But I think now everyone would agree it has been healthy talking about Emma and reflecting about her impact on all of us.

Grief expert Dr. Stephen Fleming calls legacy building part of the post-traumatic growth period, or putting something good back in the world instead of wallowing in pain.

Dr. Fleming suggests bereaved parents ask three questions as they build out the deceased child's legacy:

1. What lessons for living has the deceased child taught me?

2. What lessons about loving have I learned?

3. How am I different as a result of knowing and loving the deceased?

"Parents stay connected to the deceased by answering and reviewing these questions," Dr. Fleming says.

Creating a legacy for a deceased child should be a personal healing process. There is no right or wrong way to do it, and it should be based on what feels most meaningful and comforting to you and your family as you navigate the grieving process.

Ultimately, the best way to honour a child who has died is to keep their memory alive and to find ways to make a positive impact in the world in their name.

Pulitzer Prize- and Tony Award-winning playwright John Patrick was abandoned by his parents when he was a little boy in Kentucky. This led to his delinquent youth in foster homes and boarding schools. He once said, "Pain makes man think. Thought makes man wise. Wisdom makes life endurable."

We start to think—really think—only when life is difficult, painful, and challenging, not when life is good. As C. S. Lewis says, "God whispers to us in our pleasures, speaks in our consciences, but shouts in our pains. It is his megaphone to rouse a deaf world."

And from my experience, wisdom has come from ensuring a legacy for our child. It has been an invaluable tool for aiding in the regeneration of my life after the loss of Emma.

And once the storm is over, you won't remember how you made it through, how you managed to survive. You won't even be sure, whether the storm is really over. But one thing is certain. When you come out of the storm, you won't be the same person who walked in. That's what this storm's all about.

—HARUKI MURAKAMI, INTERNATIONALLY
BEST-SELLING AUTHOR

Chapter 11

Five Key Learnings

One spring day, while walking in the Humber Valley several years after Emma's passing, I noticed the river was running faster than usual. It had rained heavily the night before, and the tributaries were obviously draining large amounts of water into the Humber River, causing the velocity to increase.

For an unexplainable reason, I stood and stared at the turbulent river. It was mesmerizing. Immediately, my thoughts turned to the turbulence in my life brought on by Emma's death. It felt like so much had drained from me—just like those tributaries draining into the Humber River.

Then other thoughts popped into my head. Instead of looking at it from the perspective of the tributaries draining, I focused on what was added to the river, helping it regenerate and flow faster. So many fish, birds, and other wildlife depend on the river and need it to regenerate, not stagnate.

As Haruki Murakami says, I had come out of my personal and painful storm, and I wasn't the same person. Would I have preferred never to have weathered that storm? Yes, of course. I hated that storm more than anything imaginable. But events, no matter how horrific, are often out of our control.

I even wonder if I'm completely out of the storm. There's still rain, but grief spikes are now fewer and farther between. There's also so much sunshine, especially with the grandchildren, Audrey and Archer at the time of publication, and our daughters who have all grown into tremendously successful, caring women.

I don't wish entry into the fraternity of the unthinkable on anyone, but I believe my experience has taught me and changed me. Some of my key learnings may be useful for other bereaved parents.

There's a misconception by many (unless you're a science geek) that the fastest moving water is on the surface of the river. Seeing eddies and water gurgling makes us think the surface is fastest. But things are not always as they appear.

It's true, the slowest moving water is next to the bottom of the river, and each successive layer of water toward the surface flows faster than the layer below it. However, the fastest moving water is not on the surface but just below it. This is because the air creates friction with the surface and slows the water slightly at the top.

Maybe one tie-in sentence here, then . . . . Like a river . . . . My five key learnings are below:

DON'T JUDGE, AND BE PATIENT. Don't judge, because we never really fully understand the journey of others, even someone as close to you as a spouse or surviving child. On the surface, bereaved parents and siblings may appear serene, like a duck gliding down the river, but in reality this façade of normality usually masks a hell of a lot of hard work behind the scenes—like a duck paddling furiously to stay in one spot on a fast-flowing river.

As stated in earlier chapters, during the first few years after Emma died, Frances and I reacted and grieved very differently. Grief is universal but it's also personally unique, like our DNA.

I often thought at the beginning of our mourning and grief— the first six months or so—that Frances's heart was broken. I didn't think anyone could cry that much.

During that period, I would sometimes get chest pains while walking. I came to think that my heart was broken, too. The difference was that I only let myself deal with the deep pain for short periods of time when I was alone; Frances openly wept before me, and occasionally in front of the girls. Mostly she mourned and revealed her intense grief when the two of us were alone.

An addendum to this key learning is patience. Patience with your spouse and other loved ones, but also with yourself. Don't rush yourself or others into doing this or that. Things unravel all in good time.

I did my best to be patient with Frances, especially in the early days. And I think I was for the most part. But I could have done better in hindsight, and I believe I am more patient today with the passage of time. With the girls, I know I could have been more patient when they were teens, especially when I was being overprotective and trying to screen the kids they hung out with and where they were most of the time. As they say, patience is a virtue—and doubly so in grief.

KEEP COMMUNICATION OPEN. When North America was developed during the seventeenth, eighteenth, and nineteenth centuries, the first communications networks were the rivers. Long before paved roads, railways, and telecommunications networks, explorers and voyageurs relied on the rivers to get them to newfound places and for trade with their newfound partners, the Indigenous Peoples. Communication has forever been an important ingredient in moving forward and building communities, countries, and economies. The same principle holds true for building a new life after the loss of a child.

The more open communication is, the better. Silence can breed resentment and misunderstanding. Opening and examining wounds can be exceedingly helpful for regeneration, if done properly. But the communication must be done with mutual respect, love, and understanding, not anger, bitterness, or by assigning blame for a tragedy nobody wanted. Therapy with professional counselling is highly recommended. Even if this, ultimately, is not for you, at least give it a try since no person is an island.

If you feel therapy doesn't work, try something else like reading, digging into online resources, and talking to compassionate and learned friends, family, and pastoral leaders. For me, as an example, I found group therapy sessions painful. That's because I've never wanted to be forced to talk on demand about Emma with strangers. Often in group therapy, revelations go around the room from person to person, which is great for most people. Not for me, though. I need to be in the proper frame of mind to talk, and sometimes that wasn't during group therapy. Instead, I found one-on-one therapy worked best for me and provided insight and tools for communicating better with Frances and others.

LEAN ON YOUR SUPPORTERS AND COMMUNITY. Building on the second learning is understanding the value and importance of community and support. Grief can be lonely and isolating, but many parents find that they are able to connect with others who have experienced similar losses. Whether that community be online or in-person, we as humans learn and grow through shared experiences, especially if those events are horrible and tragic.

Where I live, Bereaved Families of Ontario has been supporting grieving Ontarians for more than forty-five years with ten affiliate offices around Southern Ontario. BFO offers both peer-based support and online resources at no cost to those in need. Find more information about BFO at bereavedfamilies.net.

The Compassionate Friends is an international non-profit, peer-support organization that was founded in 1969 in Coventry, England. Today, The Compassionate Friends of Canada operates across the country, offering grief education, friendship, and hope for families who are grieving the death of a child of any age and from any cause. They can be found at tcfcanada.net.

These are just two organizations out there that help bereaved parents and families. Many local communities will have other support systems and people willing to help, and they are easily found. Remember, six Canadians under age fifteen die every day on average—or 2,200 every year. There are lots of parents and families struggling after the death of a child, and there is lots of help available for them.

HONOUR THE PAST, CHERISH THE PRESENT, AND TAKE HOLD OF THE FUTURE. The death of a child can be a powerful reminder of the fragility and preciousness of life.

It is tremendously important for me to continue my relationship with Emma even though our life together on Earth was severed. I will grieve until my last breath. Grief lasts forever because love lasts forever. It took me long to understand this, but I get it now. I hope others do, too. Bereaved parents should never think about "moving on" or "getting over it." If a friend or family member tries to push that, it's time for you to re-evaluate your relationship with that person, not your relationship with your lost child.

It's critical for parents to appreciate and cherish the moments they have with loved ones, and to prioritize the things that truly matter in life. Remember, we can't change the past, but we can choose paths for the future. A path of hope and happiness, in my opinion, beats a path filled with morosity, melancholy, and what-could-have-beens.

And always remember that finding positive new paths and regenerating life in no way impacts your relationship with your lost child. One can still love, laugh, and live after the death of a child. Regeneration is not a synonym for closure. In fact, I think it's the opposite. I believe Emma wants the best for me and the rest of the family, and that includes lots of love, laughter, and life in our lives.

PRACTISE SELF-CARE. The need for self-care and self-compassion can be as essential as a lifesaver for a drowning person. Grief can take a significant toll on both physical and emotional health, and parents can learn in their "life after" the importance of self-care and self-compassion. It's natural to play the "woulda, coulda, shoulda" game early on, but it's a mug's game in the long-term. Don't blame yourself or others. No one saw it coming. No one wanted it to come. Shit happens.

I am so proud of my wife for firing that therapist with the wacky ideas about blaming God and the need to burn all of Emma's clothes. Even in a weakened state, I'm proud that Frances had the temerity to recognize her need to prioritize her own well-being and to move on to find help and support from others.

You're a lot stronger than you may think, so never doubt the power of resilience, healing, and regeneration. It goes without saying the death of a child is a monumentally devastating experience, and yet many parents find strength and resilience in the face of their grief. Healing and regeneration are possible, and you can find a way to move forward.

I've also learned the importance of understanding your role following such a family tragedy. Some are lead dogs and some are strapped in behind the lead dog, doing their best to push forward, but without the overall sweeping view the lead dog has at the front.

As the father, I assumed the role of lead dog, out front setting direction and regulating speed. I've learned it's counterproductive to live with regrets, but I wished I'd done a few things differently, especially when it comes to Kasia, Amanda, and Melanie. Maybe I ignored or misunderstood their input on the direction and speed that the family was travelling, or maybe they were never comfortable expressing such things. I don't know. What I do know is that as lead dog, I took the family over some bumps that could have been avoided.

These key learnings—and other advice sprinkled throughout this book—can be difficult to implement. They may even sound impossible, depending on where you are in your grief journey. But nothing is impossible. We can always find a sense of purpose in life and move forward in a way that honours the memory of our children who are gone.

As Martin Luther King Jr. advises when undertaking any worthy endeavour, you don't need to see the top of the staircase to take that first step.

To live is to suffer, to survive is to find
some meaning in the suffering.

— FRIEDRICH NIETZSCHE

Don't cry because it's over,
smile because it happened.

— THEODOR SEUSS GEISEL, AKA DR. SEUSS

Chapter 12

You've Still Gotta Live

Losing a child is not unique or even rare. But it is a loss like no other. And it does not discriminate. Parents from all walks of life enter the fraternity of the unthinkable every day.

Parents who have lost a child include the rich and powerful (Bill Gates, Nike founder Phil Knight), presidents and prime ministers (Joe Biden, Teddy Roosevelt, Pierre Trudeau), actors (Paul Newman, Keanu Reeves, John Travolta, Pierce Brosnan, Sylvester Stallone), musicians (Eric Clapton, Robert Plant, Roy Orbison), literary greats (Toni Morrison, Sylvia Plath), and average folk (me, you). It's a very long list with only a handful mentioned here.

No parent should ever have to go through the horrid task of burying a child, but regardless of how famous someone might be, it doesn't shield them from experiencing such a heartbreaking tragedy.

Over the past fifty years, parental bereavement has moved from the shadows—from parents suffering in silence and not talking about lost children—to today where the stigma (and sometimes social ostracization) is whitling away as more and more people understand bereaved parents want to talk about their child and their grief journeys.

For bereaved parents, there's nothing in their grief that they should be ashamed of or embarrassed about. I love Emma as much as ever, as much as any parent loves their living child. The biggest difference is Emma's earthly life ended too soon and talking about her continues to be somewhat of a taboo in our culture.

Sadly, despite raised awareness toward mental health issues, our culture still isn't great when it comes to hearing about children who are gone too soon. Too many people feel uncomfortable or awkward when bereaved parents talk about their child years later. Tears really make some uncomfortable. I have felt it and still feel it.

But I ask myself: so what? Just because hearing me talk about Emma might make somebody uncomfortable, it doesn't make Emma matter any less to me.

The fraternity of the unthinkable is a crappy club that I can never leave.

Ironically, like "good grief," which I mentioned in Chapter 9, this club may also be a silver lining to our loss because it is a place filled with remarkable and selfless people. People like

George and Kata Demeter and so many others I've met along the way.

Over the twenty-five-plus years of my grief journey, I am often struck by the immediate bond between bereaved parents. A mere look, glance, or word, and strangers instantly become kindreds. It's a spontaneous bond between people who understand the heartbreak of the death of a child. It's a pain we suffer for a lifetime, and only those who have walked the path of child loss truly understand the depth and breadth of both the pain and the love we carry.

And yet we all wish we could jump ship—that we could have met some other way, any other way. These heartbroken, shining souls are the most compassionate, empathetic, grounded, loving, brave movers and shakers you'll likely ever meet. I know the ones I've met are like that.

I've heard it said the only truly selfless people in the world are those who are faced with a terminal illness and parents who've lost a child. I tend to agree.

Show me a bereaved parent, and I'll show you someone who has likely moved mountains in honour of their child gone too soon. They start grassroot movements like MADD and Compassionate Friends. And sometimes they get laws changed for fentanyl and other killer drugs, gun control, better education, and cancer awareness and prevention for children.

They transform their grief into a force to be reckoned with. They turn their deep loss into legacy. For me, this transformation came through the Emma Johnston Memorial Fund, but some do so much more to turn into warrior activists. Why? We all want to put love back in the world where we experienced loss. And we all hope that if even one parent can be spared from joining this awful club, it makes it all worthwhile.

It's important to remember that grief is a deeply personal and individual experience, and there is no one-size-fits-all way to overcome the loss of a child. But, from my experience, those parents who actively try to put good in the world after their loss do better in moving forward and regenerating a life without their loved one.

Regaining true and deep happiness since the death of Emma has been a long and difficult process. But I truly believe Emma wants her mother and father to be happy. And we are for the most part. But it's taken a long time to get here, at least for me. This is one father who has been bent, broken, and displaced, but hopefully into a better shape and place.

Imagine Emma: I do every day and plan to continue to do so forever. After reading this book, I hope you can imagine Emma, too. There is a new, regenerated life ahead for bereaved parents. A life—not without grief—that can be filled with more joy and deep love than you might think possible at the moment.